BREATHE LIFE INTO YOUR LIFE STORY

How to Write a Story People Will Want to Read

DAWN AND MORRIS THURSTON

ILLUSTRATIONS BY AMY HADLEY

Salt Lake City • Signature Books • 2007

Cover design by Ron Stucki

Breathe Life into Your Life Story was printed on acid-free paper and was composed, printed, and bound in the United States of America.

www.signaturebooks.com

12 11 10 09 08 07   6 5 4 3 2 1

Library of Congress Cataloging-in-Publication Data
Thurston, Dawn, 1947-
    Breathe life into your life story : how to write a story people will want to read / by Dawn and Morris Thurston ; illustrations by Amy Hadley.
        Includes bibliographical references and index.
        ISBN 1-56085-094-9 (978-1-56085-094-6 : alk. paper)
    1. Autobiography—Authorship.   I. Thurston, Morris Ashcroft, 1943-   II. Title.
CT25.T49 2007
808'.06692—dc22
                                    2007007764

BREATHE LIFE
INTO YOUR
LIFE STORY

To our students.
Without them, this book
could not have been written.

Contents

*"If you would not be forgotten
as soon as you are dead,
either write things worth reading
or do things worth writing."*

—Benjamin Franklin

Introduction

With the blossoming of family history as a national hobby, more people than ever are coming to understand the importance of writing their own story. Most of these would-be authors are not typical memoir writers—the wealthy, the celebrated, or the literati—but everyday people writing about everyday experiences.

If you are reading this introduction, chances are that you, too, have thought about writing your life story. Perhaps you are a member of the "Greatest Generation" and want your children to understand and remember the values that shaped your life. Or maybe you are a "Baby Boomer" who is reaching retirement age and finding you have an abundance of memories and time to record them. Possibly you have been inspired by the remarkable number of best-selling memoirs published about ordinary lives.

Many of the "everyday folks" who try to compose their life stories have had little writing experience since leaving school, and it usually shows. Too many of them manage to turn interesting lives into uninteresting life stories because they lack the skill to do otherwise. Typically, the problem isn't the *content* of their stories; it's the way they tell them. There's a huge difference between merely recording the facts of a life and shaping those facts into a compelling narrative.

We all know people who are born storytellers and can make the most mundane experiences seem like enchanting adventures. We envy the spell they cast on their listeners, who seem to hang onto their every word. It's a gift, you may say. Perhaps … but writing an interesting story also involves skills that you can learn, practice, and apply.

This volume will introduce you to those skills. Written for novices and more experienced writers alike, it presents techniques long used by fiction writers to craft compelling characters, places, and stories. It shows how to apply these techniques to writing an unforgettable narrative.

For example, you will learn how to:

- *Show* rather than *tell*.

- Animate the people in your story so they become believable, interesting characters.

- Re-create your world so readers can visualize places, styles, and attitudes, as they were in "your day."

- Write at the gut level, revealing how your experiences affected you, and infusing your story with warmth and humanity.

- Keep your readers turning pages by applying the techniques used by suspense writers.

- Begin with a bang, with an opening that makes readers think, *This is going to be a great story!*

We have long believed that life stories written about everyday people can be as absorbing as novels. You'll find here ways to expand your vision of what *your* life story can

There's a huge difference between merely recording the facts of your life and shaping those facts into a compelling narrative.

be. We have taught these techniques for years to people who have attended our classes and seminars, and we have had the satisfaction of seeing many of our students blossom into wonderful writers. We have seen them grow to the point that they can create fascinating, inspiring narratives for their posterity or even the general public. A number of them consistently win prizes in international writing competitions. You will find two of these award-winning stories in Appendix D.

An important feature of this volume is our *Learn by Doing* exercises found in each chapter. These writing prompts are not intended to be busy work. If you complete each exercise, you will have a tremendous start on your life story. The exercises introduce new ideas, skills, and approaches that will spark your creativity and nudge you out of doing things in the same old way.

> *"I find that the harder I work, the more luck I seem to have."*
> —Thomas Jefferson

It's obvious to most people that they can't learn to play the piano or master an athletic skill simply by reading a book about it. The same principle applies to writing. *We learn by doing.* For ease of reference, we have repeated the exercises all in one place as Appendix 1.

If you are the kind of person who likes to read a book quickly, we encourage you to start over again when you've finished and read this one a second time at a measured pace, alternating reading with writing. Your life story won't be written in one sitting, but if you keep at it, you will be richly rewarded.

As you write, we encourage you to practice what we preach. It may mean the difference between a life story that languishes on a dusty bookshelf and one that thrusts itself into your readers' hearts.

Chapter 1

Breathing Lessons

First Things First

*N*o one intends to write a lifeless life story. Yet many do. We've all had interesting experiences, visited interesting places, known interesting people. No one lacks for story material. So, how does a fascinating life lose its luster and vitality on the way to the printed page? What makes the difference between a page-turner and a dreary disappointment? It may be obvious, but worth stating even so: It's all in the way the story is told.

Some life stories aren't fashioned as stories at all, but merely as a string of names, dates, places, and events arranged into sentences. You may be familiar with the type. We call them "pedigree chart" stories. They usually start out something like this: "I was born on March 4, 1935, in Newton, Middlesex County, Massachusetts, the first child and only daughter of James and Ethel Miller Wallace. My father was born in Boston, Suffolk County, Massachusetts, on October 15, 1902 ..." And so they continue, sterile and fact-heavy, like encyclopedia entries, describing what the author *did*, but not who she *was*.

You may have inherited a family history like this from a relative. These kinds of books serve a purpose as historical records, but they tend to end up mostly unread—stashed away on a dusty bookshelf because they fail to tell a story that engages the reader's interest.

Life narratives don't have to be dry as dust. The recent wave of best-selling memoirs demonstrates that even stories about ordinary people can keep readers enthralled and turning pages like the most compelling fiction. If you've read Frank McCourt's Pulitzer Prize-winning *Angela's Ashes*—more than a year on the bestseller lists—or Rick Bragg's *All Over but the Shoutin'*, or Mary Karr's *The Liar's Club*, you understand the power of a well-written memoir about everyday people.

Of course, many of the best-sellers were written by pros—writers who have honed their skills through years of practice. Their stories resonate with us because the authors re-create people, places, and events in a way that helps us visualize what it was like to be them, to know their friends and to live in their communities, to be in their shoes.

How do they do this? They borrow techniques from fiction writers. They craft compelling beginnings, both for their books and for each chapter. They make their family and friends recognizable as real people, not just as names on the page. They bring to life the towns where they lived and worked, showing what things were like in their day. They engage our emotions by telling stories that reveal tension and conflict. They write with candor and honesty.

You can use these same techniques to breathe life into your story—even if you haven't written anything since high school or college, even if you're only writing a little something for your kids and grandkids. We've learned that people of all levels of education and experience can write a story that is captivating and illuminating.

Each of the following chapters will introduce you to different techniques that can help you flesh out your memories and bring them onto the page. By reading excerpts we've included from published memoirs and autobiographies, you'll see how other authors have used the same techniques to enhance their stories. Finally, you'll find writing prompts— *Learn by Doing* exercises—that will help you apply what you've learned.

We recognize that writing can produce more than a little anxiety, particularly if you have not had much experience at it.

Don't worry.

The *quality* of your writing will improve with practice. Some people don't realize this. They understand the need for practice to master an athletic skill or a musical instrument, but they don't always associate the same principle with developing writing proficiency. They think the ability to produce beautiful prose is a gift—something you either have or you don't. When it doesn't come easy for them, they think they lack the talent for it and give up. It's true, some people are born writers, but they, too, have to work hard at their craft, reworking their sentences, polishing, sometimes chucking it all in the wastebasket and starting afresh. It rarely comes easy for anyone. (Notice how the quotes from

"When I face the desolate impossibility of writing five hundred pages, a sick sense of failure falls on me and I know I can never do it. This happens every time. Then gradually I write one page and then another. One day's work is all I can permit myself to contemplate and I eliminate the possibility of ever finishing."
—John Steinbeck

professional writers in the margins of this chapter validate this point.)

If you worry too much about the quality of your writing in the beginning stages, you'll cripple your creativity from the get-go.

Give yourself a chance! Be patient and trust that the more you write, the better you'll get. And you will.

A preliminary caution: Don't make it harder than it needs to be. In the chapters that follow, we'll introduce you to ways to enhance your ability to write an interesting narrative. Before you embark on what could be new territory for you, we want to stress some principles that will ease the rigors of the journey.

Breathing Management

Almost everyone has heard the Nike slogan, "Just do it!" It can be applied to any new venture, including writing. The most difficult part of your journey is getting started, so here are three principles that will help you undertake this great adventure.

Principle 1: Write it down, then fix it up

Polished prose rarely flows easily out of a writer's head. Ideas, and words to express them, can come at an excruciatingly slow pace. If you worry too much about the quality of your writing at the beginning, you'll cripple your creativity from the get-go. Write first, polish later.

At first glance, this principle may seem to contradict everything we've said to this point. You may be saying, "First they tell me to make my story interesting. Now they tell me to just get something down on paper." Bear with us a moment and you'll see where we're heading with this.

First an anecdote: Dawn was an English major in college and had to write papers for every class. She often found she spent more time writing the first paragraph than the pages that followed. Why? She was determined to write something that sang with brilliance. She'd write a sentence, then cross it out and rewrite it. She'd rearrange a few more words, then come up with a new beginning. The whole process was laborious and frustrating.

Years later, after she began writing for magazines, she discovered the reason for her difficulty: She was trying to make her first draft a final one. She was concentrating so much on the finish line, she was stumbling at the starting gate. It's a common trap, one that frequently snares inexperienced writers who second-guess every word they put on the page.

Don't worry too much at first about what "sounds good." Loosen up. Give yourself permission to write a lousy first draft. What does this mean? It means you begin by writing down anything, willy-nilly, as it comes to mind, trusting that you'll come back later and revise it the way you want it. When you return to your writing after permitting some time to pass, you'll be surprised how many new and better ideas will flow into your head. You'll cut things out, move things around, change a word or phrase, prune and polish the piece to your satisfaction.

This method, called freewriting, lets you capture new ideas as you write. Sometimes, halfway down the page, a key idea or phrase will occur to you that you'll think is perfect for your opening paragraph. It may not have come to you without first allowing yourself enough freedom to write anything that came to mind. You'll find this approach saves an enormous amount of time in the long run and produces a richer final product.

We used this method to write the first draft of this book. Our initial version wasn't very good, nor did we expect it to be. We viewed it as a work in progress, something to be pruned and polished over time.

You'll be able to write the stories you want if you allow yourself the freedom to write a lousy first draft. When you become involved in a project as extensive as a personal history, you'll find yourself constantly thinking of new ideas. You'll change your mind about how to organize and present your story. Your writing skills will improve as you go along. In the end, that awful first draft will become the interesting, well-written story you want to tell.

Principle 2: Read to learn

Authors read extensively to gather ideas about writing. They want to see how other authors handle subjects and situations similar to those they're writing about. They read to keep themselves motivated to write.

As the author of your own life story, you should find books that are similar to the one you want to write to expand your vision of what you want to accomplish. There's no better teacher than a well-written memoir that covers some of the same territory you'll be grappling with in your own project.

Read with a critical eye. Notice how the author writes about the people and places in her life. Notice how she deals with conflict and "uncomfortable subjects." Underline passages you like and analyze what makes them good. Take notes. You're a student learning how to make your writing better, so be open to new ideas.

Here are a few memoirs and autobiographies we recom-

"I love writing at a gallop because it leaves my internal critic behind."
—Virginia Woolf

mend for their superb writing. You'll find excerpts from many of them in the chapters that follow, illustrating the techniques we cover in this book.

- Angelou, Maya. *I Know Why the Caged Bird Sings.* New York: Bantam, 1993.

- Baker, Russell. *Growing Up.* New York: Congden & Weed, 1982.

- Bragg, Rick. *All Over but the Shoutin'.* New York: Pantheon, 1997.

- Bragg, Rick. *Ava's Man.* New York: Knopf, 2001.

- Cantwell, Mary. *Manhattan When I Was Young.* New York: Penguin, 1995.

- Carter, Jimmy. *An Hour before Daylight.* Simon & Schuster, 2001.

- Conway, Jill Ker. *The Road from Coorain.* New York: Vintage, 1989.

- Dillard, Annie. *An American Childhood.* New York: Harper-Collins, 1998.

- Frazier, Ian. *Family.* New York: Farrar, Straus, Giroux, 1994.

- James, P. D. *A Time to Be in Earnest: A Fragment of Autobiography.* New York: Knopf, 1999.

- Karr, Mary. *The Liar's Club.* New York: Vintage, 1996.

- McCourt, Frank. *Angela's Ashes.* New York: Scribner, 1996.

- Wolff, Tobias. *This Boy's Life.* New York: Grove Press, 1989.

Principle 3: Beware of the HU-M-I virus

Over the years, we've led hundreds of students through the life story writing process. They often begin as excited as

"Rewriting is like scrubbing the basement floor with a tooth brush."
—Pete Murphy

Little Leaguers at the season opener. By the second week, many succumb to the HU-M-I virus. Here is the symptom: a deflated self-perception that causes them to ask, WHO AM I to write my life story—because

- My life is not worth writing about.
- I have nothing to say.
- What I write sounds trite and boring.
- My family won't be interested in reading this.
- I don't know correct grammar and punctuation.
- I haven't written anything in years.
- I don't know how to get started.
- I don't remember much of my life.
- People will think I'm arrogant.
- I've made a lot of mistakes I can't write about.
- I'll never finish it.
- I'm no good at this.

Do any of these sound familiar? Perhaps you won't relate to all of these feelings, but some will undoubtedly ring true. If you struggle with self-doubts, welcome to the club! We can tell you, as we do all our students, that this is a universal contagion, afflicting at times the best of writers. And here's our diagnosis: *It's all in your head!*

That's right. It's a phantom virus, for which we offer a three-part remedy:

1. Ignore the noise in your head.
2. Trust your heart.
3. Get your feet wet.

That's it. We've been at this long enough to know that if you follow our prescription, you'll begin to feel energized and will keep the virus at bay.

Never forget that your decision to write is a good one, that it can yield tremendous emotional satisfaction. Soon after beginning our writing courses, students begin to say things like: "I can't sleep at night. My mind is buzzing with memories from my childhood." "My life will never be the same." "I don't read the way I used to. I keep analyzing the author's writing style."

"I don't think anyone should write their autobiography until after they're dead."
—Samuel Goldwyn

As you recall and write about your experiences, you'll find your life changing as well. You'll suddenly remember events you haven't thought about in years. Your life will take on new meaning as you develop fresh insights about your experiences. You'll feel pride in your accomplishments and see personal growth in the challenges you faced. You'll find at times that you are unable to get words onto the page fast enough.

We've devoted the majority of this first chapter to issues that need to be considered up front: identifying and dismissing the hurdles, or at least finding ways around them. We've offered tools to get you started and to simplify the process.

Now we'll show you how to make your story *interesting*.

Learn by Doing

1. Draw a simple floor plan of your childhood home. If you lived in more than one home, choose the one that was most meaningful to you. First, roughly sketch the exterior walls, then draw in the rooms. Now, begin adding little boxes to represent furniture. Where was your couch located? Your bed? Your kitchen table? Your Christmas tree? Now sketch in the driveway, the garage, prominent trees and shrubs, the tire swing, and so on. (See Appendix B for an example.) You'll find this exercise will resurrect all kinds of memories.

Now, while these thoughts are still fresh in your mind, write a description of this house. Begin with a simple sentence like, "When I was a child, I lived at (fill in address)." Now continue freewriting about that home, including details as they come to you. Don't be content to merely describe the house. Tell how you felt about it. Describe memorable activities that occurred there. If your writing veers off on a tangent, go with it. Later you will come back to this assignment to edit and shape it to your needs. Don't be discouraged if you feel you haven't said what you want to say. You are learning and you will improve with practice.

2. Begin reading a memoir or autobiography that will give you ideas for writing your own life story. (See page 11 for some of our recommendations.) If the book is one you have purchased, underline passages you particularly like. Analyze them to determine what makes them good. Make notes to yourself. Use the book as a training manual. Don't read it all in one sitting. Intersperse your writing with reading. Read the book when you want to relax—when you feel too fatigued to write.

Chapter 2

The Power of "Showing"

Give Your Story the Breath of Life

*D*on't just tell me that you love me—you've got to show me! You may have heard this refrain a time or two, maybe even said it yourself. Actions *do* speak louder than words.

The principle is as important to writing as it is to good relationships. In most cases, showing *is* better than telling. Too many stories seem flat and monotonous because their authors do too much telling.

When you summarize and generalize, you suck the life out of your stories. If you limit your description of an important experience to a cursory summary like "I graduated from Harvard during the turbulent '60s. It was an interesting time to be there," not only do you miss the opportunity to engage your readers with a compelling narrative, you keep them at arm's length. When you simply describe your grandfather as "a generous man of unflagging integrity," you pay him a compliment but do him a disservice because your general statement doesn't make him live for your readers. It

15

doesn't capture his humanity or convince the reader your grandfather is who you say he is.

Telling? Showing? How are they different? To understand their applications in writing, let's look at a few examples. In the paragraph below, a writer describes her grandmother. Does she tell or show?

> Though my grandmother showered me with affection, she was not as generous with other people in her life, particularly the neighbors who shared her apartment building. Grandma was a bit of a snob, really. My visits with her were always peppered with snooty observations about this or that neighbor she deemed unworthy of her friendship. I was always amused by her keen observations of others' foibles. She missed nothing, and she forgave nothing.

We learn from this example that Grandma is critical and patronizing, but only because the author has *told* us she is. It's not bad writing for starters because the author is quite specific and even colorful in telling us about a particular character trait. But if we are really to know Grandma—to visualize her as a real person—the author needs to show her in action, show her being spiteful and critical of others. Notice how the following example, written by one of our students, *shows* us the woman that was only summarized in the previous paragraph.

> "Gussie is not my friend," Grandma said indignantly. "We have nothing in common. My friends and I play bridge for matchsticks. Gussie likes to play poker for money. She won't eat in restaurants unless they're kosher. She won't wear anything but house dresses. She can hardly read, so she gossips

about everybody. Sometimes I hate her. Just because you know somebody a long time, just because you rented the third floor of her house, just because your husband worked for her husband … doesn't make you friends."[1]

Now here Grandma has become more real—petty, sniping, and revealing herself through her own words. The author hasn't just *told* us about Grandma, she's *shown* her engaging in the sort of behavior that made her memorable to her granddaughter.

Unless you want people in your story to appear dull and lifeless, resist the temptation to summarize their personalities and characteristics. Show them speaking and interacting with each other. Let your readers observe their behavior so they can form their own judgments about them.

Show through Description

Learn to write in a way that paints such vivid pictures, readers will be able to see or hear, or even smell and feel what it is you're describing. The illustrations on page 18 show how it's done. In the first example, the statement on the left makes a bland, vague observation about the relationship between a dog and its owner. The description in the right column, on the other hand, *shows* us that relationship by giving the dog a physical presence and a personality. We can visualize the scene and feel the emotion of the moment because the description shows rather than tells.

In the second example, we learn details about Wilhelm's dress and behavior that let us see the eccentricity for ourselves. Wilhelm becomes a memorable flesh-and-bones individual who would enliven any story. In the summary statement on the left, he's merely a name on the page.

"Good writing is supposed to evoke sensation in the reader—not the fact that it is raining, but the feeling of being rained upon."
—E. L. Doctorow

Telling	Showing
My dog had a way of cheering me up.	I arrived home tired and deflated. I walked to the door, and as I pushed the key into the lock, I could see through the window that Emma was crouching in anticipation on the other side. I threw open the door and she leaped out and danced on her hind legs, trying desperately to jump into my arms, though she knew it was impossible so long as I stood upright. I bent and picked her up. A fluffy mound of excitement, she immediately began licking my face. After a moment or two, I set her on the floor. She began racing around me as I walked down the hallway, just waiting to spring into my lap wherever I sat down. I smiled despite myself, and suddenly things didn't seem so bad.
Telling	**Showing**
Some people considered Uncle Wilhelm an eccentric.	I arrived at my Uncle Wilhelm's cabin wearing my paint-smeared cutoffs, torn t-shirt, and battered tennis shoes, ready for our hike up the mountainside. Wilhelm appeared at the door looking like a Teutonic dandy in his tan lederhosen, green embroidered shirt, red scarf, brown knee socks, and high-topped hiking boots. I was not at all surprised when he picked up a carved oak walking stick and, after dramatically filling his lungs with the mountain air, announced, "Let us depart for the high country!"

Below is a third illustration. Read the *telling* example and ask yourself how you might dramatize the feelings of the young woman toward her mother. Then read the *showing* example to see how it can be done.

Your life story will include descriptions and scenes involving people, places, feelings, events, and more. Constantly analyze your writing to see if you've included sufficient

Telling	Showing
When I was a teenager, I had an adversarial relationship with my mother and longed to escape from her implied criticisms.	As I entered the kitchen, my mother turned from her mixing bowl and eyed me with the same expression I had seen her use when inspecting an overripe tomato. "You look nice, dear," she said.
	I was silent, hoping that Roger would soon arrive and rescue me.
	"Your hair is in your eyes—would you like to borrow my clip?" Mother was smiling, but it was a hollow, shallow smile, one that said, you can't seriously be thinking of going out like that!
	"Aren't you afraid of catching a chill? I'm sure you would feel better with a jacket to cover your shoulders. You know, that top seems a little tight. Wouldn't you rather wear your blue one?"
	She continued to talk, but I forced myself to keep a blank look on my face and wait for freedom to march up our front walk and ring the doorbell.

detail. Are you *showing* enough so your readers can visualize what you're trying to communicate?

Showing Conveys Truth

Besides making your story more interesting and compelling, *showing* makes it more believable. By *showing*, you support your case that your brother was a brat and your mother a saint. When you generalize and summarize, you essentially tell your reader, "This is how it was because I say so." Readers need proof. They like to form their own opinions based on the evidence you present.

For example, one of our adult students demonstrated his writing ability through several short writing exercises and decided he was ready to write a full life story. His first effort was a lengthy sketch of his youth. One personality dominated the story—his father. Whenever the student mentioned him, it was in a negative tone. It was clear the student harbored a great deal of resentment toward his father.

When the class finished reading his story, we found ourselves strangely unmoved by the descriptions of his father's failings. In fact, we felt an odd compulsion to come to the father's defense. Why couldn't we feel the same anger against the man the author felt?

"You haven't lived with the man like I did," said the student.

But this answer was too easy. After all, many great novels provoke strong negative feelings toward some characters even though they are wholly fictional. Certainly a memoir, based on real life, could do the same.

After mulling it over, we came up with the reason: We were never *shown* enough of the father's behavior to be convinced that the father was as bad as the author said he was. Instead of telling us about his father's deflating sarcasm, the author needed to include some dialogue so we could hear him belittle his wife and children—so we, too, could be affected by this behavior. We needed to see the other obnoxious traits that had estranged him from his son. Without showing us the proof, the author had failed to elicit our sympathy or interest.

In his memoir, *Angela's Ashes,* Frank McCourt paints a picture of a childhood in Limerick, Ireland, amid such impoverished, squalid conditions, it's a miracle he survived them. A large part of the blame for his situation can be placed squarely on the shoulders of McCourt's feckless, alcoholic father. So here we have another father who provoked bitterness in his son, but in this case McCourt shows us the man and we understand the son's feelings.

> Dad is stumbling up the stairs, making a speech about how we all have to die for Ireland. He lights a match and touches it to the candle by Mam's bed. He holds the candle over his head and marches around the room singing....
>
> Michael wakes and lets out a loud cry, the Hannons are banging on the wall next door, Mam is telling Dad he's a disgrace and why doesn't he get out of the house altogether.
>
> He stands in the middle of the floor with the candle over his head. He pulls a penny from his pocket and waves it to Malachy and me. Your Friday Penny, boys, he says. I want you to jump out of that bed and line up here like two soldiers and promise to die for Ireland and I'll give the two of you the Friday Penny.

"Don't say the old lady screamed ... bring her on and let her scream."
—Mark Twain

If a writer does not show us his suffering, he will not elicit either sympathy or interest.

Malachy sits up in bed. I don't want it, he says.

And I tell him I don't want it, either.

Dad stands for a minute, swaying, and puts the penny back in his pocket. He turns toward Mam and she says, You're not sleeping in this bed tonight. He makes his way downstairs with the candle, sleeps on a chair, misses work in the morning, loses the job at the cement factory and we're back on the dole again.[2]

McCourt could merely have told us that his father was an incorrigible alcoholic who embarrassed his family, repeatedly lost his job, and kept his children worrying about where they'd get their next meal. Instead, he shows us the man reeling up the stairs, singing, talking, and disgusting his wife and children. With all this evidence, we too react to him with the strongest of feelings.

In the chapters that follow, we will return often to the principle of *showing*. It's an important part of breathing life into your characters, creating vivid settings, communicating powerful emotions, and convincing the reader that what you say is true.

Notes

1. Excerpt from the story, "Mrs. Sachs," written by our student Bonnie Copeland of Costa Mesa, California.

2. Frank McCourt, *Angela's Ashes* (New York: Scribner, 1996), 111-12.

Learn by Doing

3. Identify a person for whom you feel (or felt) romantic affection. List two or three one-word attributes that draw you to this person. For example, the individual may be kind, funny, cheerful, attractive, affectionate, intelligent, etc. Re-create an incident involving this person where these attributes are demonstrated. Avoid summary statements like "Jeremy was a cheerful man." Instead, show Jeremy's cheerfulness.

4. Identify a time in your life when you felt afraid. Write about how you felt, describing how your body reacted to the incident. What were your thoughts at the time? How did you behave? Show us your feelings, don't just tell about them. For example, you could describe how you used to duck your head and wish you were elsewhere whenever your mother took you to her hometown and introduced you to her friends and relatives. Or you could dramatize the time you were struck speechless when you suddenly came face to face with the boy you had dreamed about since the first day of school. Or you could let your readers feel your terror when you were asked to deliver a short speech in history class. Describe how the sweat ran down your armpits and your voice trembled, compounding your embarrassment by broadcasting your fear.

5. Instead of reporting that you grew up in a "small town," take your readers for a walk. Visit the country store and describe the tall glass jars filled with colorful hard candy that attracted you as a child. Look in on the four-room schoolhouse and tell about the classes that consisted of students in several different grade levels. Describe how you could visit any of your friends in town in a few minutes' walk. Write about the telephone operator who knew the names—and much of the business—of every family in town. (Chapter 6 offers more ideas for writing about places.)

5-19

SOMETIMES, WHEN YOU ARE A GREAT WRITER, THE WORDS COME SO FAST YOU CAN HARDLY PUT THEM DOWN ON PAPER...

SOMETIMES

Chapter 3

Lights, Camera, Action!

Zoom in on Key Events

*W*e love going to the movies. It's entertaining and relaxing to sit in a darkened theater and escape from our worries while we watch other people's lives dramatized on the Big Screen. As the characters struggle with problems and inter-act with each other, we often feel as though we know them. They seem so *real*. That is the seductive charm of movies.

Let's say that one Friday night we go to a movie adver-tised to be about the Civil War. Our expectations high, we sit in the theater munching popcorn, waiting to be trans-ported back to 1860s America. Instead, when the lights dim, a distinguished-looking actor appears on the screen against a plain white background. He stands behind a podium, looks directly into the camera, and in a sonorous voice an-nounces, "This film is about the Civil War. The year is 1861 and Abraham Lincoln is President of the United States. The war began over the issue of slavery. It was the North against the South...." Suppose the movie slogs along in this vein all

25

the way to its conclusion, the actor tediously reciting facts about the war.

We were expecting to be transported back to that time in history, to see soldiers fighting on smoky battlefields, to hear the crack and boom of gunfire, to *feel* what it was like to be in the heat of battle. What happened to the dramatic scenes that could bring this story to life?

Boooo! We want a refund!

Of course, the film we've described doesn't exist, but we can imagine being trapped in a theater for two hours watching someone relate facts about the Civil War. The point is this: Merely telling what happened makes for an uneventful story in any media. *Scenes,* on the other hand, bring events to life, whether they are stories made into movies or stories made into books.

Instead of simply summarizing your experiences like the narrator of our fictional movie, why not try a creative approach? Borrow a technique from Hollywood and intersperse your narrative with dramatic incidents from your life. Resurrect some of those sad, funny, poignant, and frightening moments from your past and re-create conversations, behavior, and emotions as you remember them.

For many of you, this may be new territory. Unless you've taken creative writing classes or have a particular bent for fiction writing, you may feel intimidated about trying the more inventive form of written expression required to construct a dramatic scene. Most people have had more practice with expository writing—the kind of writing required in school for term papers and in the workplace to create memos and business reports. Unfortunately, when used exclusively to reconstruct the story of your life, it results in lifeless characters and a lackluster rendering of an interesting life.

If you lack experience with creative writing, it doesn't mean you can't learn something new. Most students who enroll in our classes begin with the assumption that they will simply summarize their experiences on paper. When we show them how to bring people and incidents to life on the page, they become converted—particularly after they practice and develop their skills in this form of writing. We continually marvel at what accomplished writers people can become when they are open to new ideas and are willing to practice. This chapter will give you the groundwork you need so you can invigorate your stories with compelling scenes.

"When in doubt, have a man come through the door with a gun in his hand."
—Raymond Chandler

Summary vs. Scene

Now let's return again to our Civil War example to examine the difference between exposition and the style of writing required to craft a scene. For this exercise we'll look at examples from two sources: the *Encyclopedia Americana* and Margaret Mitchell's *Gone with the Wind*.

Both focus on the same topic: the devastation and loss of life that occurred in the battle for Atlanta. However, each example approaches the subject differently, producing substantially different results. Let's first examine an excerpt from the encyclopedia:

> Gen. William T. Sherman's Union army fought its way through the battles of Dalton, Resaca Kingston, New Hope Church, and Kennesaw Mountain to the outskirts of Atlanta. The Federals repulsed

Confederate counterattacks northwest and east of Atlanta, then forced the defenders from the city after a victory at Jonesboro. The key city of the Deep South was taken. In the campaign the Federals lost 4,428 killed, 22,882 wounded and 4,442 missing. Confederate losses were 3,044 killed, 21,996 wounded, and 12,983 missing.[1]

This paragraph, an example of expository writing, presents a great deal of information and covers a broad expanse of time in a short amount of space. This is what exposition does well. But while this excerpt satisfies our need for facts and figures, it doesn't make us feel what it was like to live through that experience. It maintains an emotional distance. It *tells* what it was like, but it doesn't *show* us.

Notice below how Margaret Mitchell's description of the same events offers a different perspective. Mitchell doesn't try to provide a history of the entire campaign. She doesn't say anything about most of the famous battles associated with the fall of Atlanta. Rather, she zooms in on one specific individual, Scarlet O'Hara, and one specific moment in time.

> She pushed her way swiftly through the crowds, past the packed hysterical mob surging in the open space of Five Points, and hurried as fast as she could down the short block toward the depot. Through the tangle of ambulances and the clouds of dust, she could see doctors and stretcher bearers bending, lifting, hurrying…. As she rounded the corner of the Atlanta Hotel and came in full view of the depot and the tracks she halted, appalled.
>
> Lying in the pitiless sun, shoulder to shoulder, head to feet, were hundreds of wounded men, lining the tracks, the sidewalks stretched out in end-

less rows under the car shed. Some lay stiff and still but many writhed under the hot sun, moaning. Everywhere swarms of flies hovered over the men, crawling and buzzing in their faces, everywhere the blood, dirty bandages, groans, screamed curses of pain as stretcher bearers lifted men.[2]

Rather than giving us facts and statistics, Mitchell thrusts us into the action, so we find ourselves walking alongside Scarlet O'Hara, seeing through her eyes, hearing through her ears. The encyclopedia gives us detailed historical background, but Mitchell seizes our emotions and demands our attention. Who could resist reading further?

What Makes a Scene?

To better illustrate the difference between summary and scene, let's examine what happens when an expository sentence is transformed into a scene.

Here's the summary sentence:

"I was born on November 28, 1933, in Springfield, Illinois, in the height of the Great Depression—one more mouth for my unemployed father to feed."

Now, here's the scene:

"Either make yourself useful, Harry, or get out of here," Aunt Emma shouted at my father on the day I was born. Dad glared at his sister a moment, then seeing she meant business, he tossed his newspaper on the floor and began collecting dirty dishes from the kitchen table.

Amid all his clumsy clattering, Dad and Aunt Emma heard a baby cry and looked toward the ceiling, in the direction of the sound. "Looks like you got yourself another mouth to feed, little brother," Aunt Emma said, shaking her head as Dad trudged up the stairs toward the bedroom.

It was November 28, 1933, in Springfield, Illinois, the middle of the Great Depression. Dad was out of work, and I had come howling into his life, his eighth child in twelve years.

What makes this example a scene?

• It focuses on a specific moment in time, not a generalized time frame.

• It includes people talking to each other and exhibiting different kinds of behavior.

• It reveals personalities through what these people say and do, not from what the author says about them.

Taking Dramatic License

Good scenes contain all kinds of details that help readers visualize what is occurring—details that may cause some writers to squirm. For example, how does the author of the previous scene *know* what was said and done by his father and aunt on the day he was born? Obviously he doesn't, though he may have learned something about the incident from one of his relatives. He may have known his aunt thought his father was foolish and incompetent. He may even have heard his aunt's sarcasm as he grew up, so it was easy for him to imagine her berating his father.

Some writers hesitate to take the liberty required to recreate a conversation they may not have witnessed or remember exactly. (Who can remember exactly what was said in *any* conversation?) They're cautious because they feel readers will question their integrity as writers if they add details they can't document. They worry about putting words in peoples' mouths and offending living relatives. They prefer to adhere to the facts as they remember them.

The reality is that the authors of all the best memoirs take dramatic license of some sort—and we all know it, although we likely don't think about it very much. Most memoirs contain conversations the author can't possibly remember verbatim unless someone recorded them. Nor can the author recall exactly all the details of incidents that occurred years before, details she inserts in her scene to make it more vivid for her readers. We understand this, trusting the author has probably done her best to recall the event as honestly as she can.

Memory is an illusive thing. So is truth. Different family members can experience the same event and describe what happened in different ways. Which account captures the truth?

Even our own recollection of events changes over time, as does our understanding of those events. Our experiences continually shape our view of our lives and ourselves. If we had written our life story ten years ago, it probably would be a different story than the one we would write today. Which one would be truer? That's hard to say, for in each case we would try to capture the emotional truth of our recollections at that time.

So if you decide to add scenes to your life story to make it more interesting, you're going to have to draw upon both your memory *and* your creativity to re-create the past as you remember it. It may involve adding details you're unsure of

The reality is that authors of all the best memoirs take dramatic license of some sort— and we all know it, although we likely don't think about it very much.

to help your readers visualize the incident, but you'll likely capture the essence of what happened, and your readers will find your story far more engaging because of it.

Using Dialogue in Scenes

If your scene includes more than one person, they're probably going to talk to each other. That's good because we learn a lot about people from what they say.

There's no better way to illustrate your mother's personality than to get her talking. In the example used earlier in this chapter, we become acquainted with Aunt Emma from what she says. We learn she's industrious, a bit bossy, and exasperated with her brother. Her statements are more illuminating than if the author had simply told us, "Aunt Emma was a bossy old biddy who criticized my father for his laziness." Instead, Aunt Emma's statements allow us to deduce this information for ourselves, which is far more interesting and powerful.

Beginning writers rarely include dialogue in their memoirs. Perhaps this is because it seems easier and more natural to tell a story from our own point of view. We'd rather summarize for our readers rather than allow them to think for themselves. Maybe we are afraid they will reach the wrong conclusion. Nevertheless, when writers include dialogue in their writing, they are usually surprised at how interesting their stories have become and how much more effective they are at getting across their point of view.

When You Can't Remember What Was Said

"This is all well and good," you may be saying. "I see where dialogue could spice up my story. But I can't *remember* what was said in a conversation that occurred decades ago. There is simply no way I can use dialogue when describing a scene from my childhood."

Most of us could not accurately reproduce a conversation that took place yesterday, much less one that occurred decades ago. As we have said, authors of popular memoirs know this, but it doesn't deter them from capitalizing on the innate appeal of dialogue. They give it their best shot, knowing that their story will retain its integrity because they'll probably get it mostly right.

Examine how Pulitzer Prize-winning author Russell Baker reconstructs a conversation from his childhood in a scene from his memoir, *Growing Up*. Here he introduces us to his charismatic Uncle Harold who, Baker tells us, is an incurable liar. Harold and some relatives are playing cards in the dining room. Baker, a child at the time, is an onlooker. Downstairs in the parlor lies a man in a coffin, which is not unusual because their landlord sometimes rents the parlor to an undertaker. Uncle Harold begins the conversation by announcing that the old gentleman in the coffin did not look dead to him.

> "I could swear I saw one of his eyelids flicker," he said.
>
> Nobody paid him any attention.
>
> "You can't always be sure they're dead," he said.
>
> Nobody was interested except me.
>
> "A man I knew was almost buried alive," he said.
>
> "Are you going to play the jack or hold it all night?" my mother asked.
>
> "It was during the war," Uncle Harold said. "In

France. They were closing the coffin on him when I saw him blink one eye."

The cards passed silently and were shuffled.

"I came close to being buried alive once myself one time," he said.[3]

Would it be reasonable to believe Baker remembered exactly what was said during that card game he witnessed when he was just a kid? Of course not. Did this bother any of the millions of readers who made his story a bestseller? Did it bother the judges who awarded the book the Pulitzer Prize? Obviously not!

It's likely that Harold made quite an impression on his young nephew with his hair-raising stories. If Baker didn't re-create the conversation verbatim, he wrote words that captured the gist of what was said and the spirit of the occasion. He could simply have summarized this incident for us, but by creating a scene with dialogue he made his Uncle Hal more real and interesting.

Adding Dialogue to a Story

One of our students turned in a writing assignment in which he recalled a childhood Christmas and how disappointed he was when he did not receive the gift he hoped for. The sketch contained no dialogue. Although it covered a subject of considerable interest, it seemed flat when read aloud.

As an experiment, we asked Walter a few questions about the characters in the story. Then we analyzed the emotions that were presented, summarized them, and created an imaginary dialogue to capture what might have been said that Christmas day many years ago.

When we read our dialogue-enhanced sketch in class, everyone agreed the story was more lively than it had been. They also learned more about the characters than they had originally. However, the most interesting comment came from Walter, who said, "Strangely, your dialogue is almost exactly as I remember it."

How had we been able to create dialogue we had never heard in the first place, and the only person who had heard the original conversation endorsed it as being eerily authentic? Because we understood the circumstances, knew a little about the characters, and could imagine the essence of what might have been said. Since nobody could remember the exact words, our reconstructed dialogue seemed real.

The lesson is that although we cannot hope to duplicate precisely what was said, we can generally shoot close to the mark. So go for it. Enliven your scenes with some conversations. You'll be surprised how much more interesting and moving your story will become.

Disclaimers for the Squeamish

Writers who are skittish about making up dialogue may feel better if they protect themselves with statements like:

- Given what I remember about Mother and the incident, she probably said something like the following: "…"

- To the best of my recollection, Dad said on that occasion, "…"

- It would have been typical of Grandma Jones to say, "…"

- Uncle Jake allegedly said, "…"

If you must *occasionally* use qualifiers, go ahead. In general, however, it is better to leave out "hedge clauses" because they are implied anyway and tend to clutter the story, detracting from the feeling of immediacy in the portrait you are painting. Your readers already know your dialogue is "as you recall it" and not a verbatim transcript.

Another way to help ease your conscience about fabricated conversations is to include a disclaimer in your story's preface. For example, you could write something like this:

> The conversations included in this life history have been recreated from memory. While I do not recall exactly what was said, I have tried to capture the spirit of these occasions to illuminate the personalities of the individuals involved.

Constructing Dialogue

The thing is, if you taped a conversation and transcribed it verbatim, it wouldn't make good reading. It would probably contain uninteresting small talk and half-finished sentences, things no one would care about. The dialogue you create should sound like natural speech, but it should be stripped of the non-essential blathering that fills most conversations. Each utterance should do useful work in moving the story along, establishing the emotional tone of the incident or illuminating something about the people in the story. So avoid fluff like:

"Hi, how are you?"

"Just fine, thank you."

"You're looking well."

Such statements add nothing to your scenes. Watch, though, that you don't make your characters sound stilted and stuffy by filling their speech with too much useful information, called "information dropping." Also be aware that most people don't speak in complete sentences. We speak in fragments. We use slang. We interrupt each other. Remember these things when you construct conversations. The people in your scenes should sound natural, like themselves.

Dialogue is often the most important part of a scene. To get it right, you may want to do some research. Listen to conversations around you and notice how people talk. Read passages of dialogue in novels to see how it's constructed and what's revealed about the plot, setting, and characters through what people say and do as they're talking to each other.

Most important, practice! Write out some lines, then read them aloud to see how they sound. Ask others to read them aloud. Your ear will be your best judge of whether or not it sounds natural.

Finally, ask yourself whether your dialogue advances some goal you have for writing the scene in the first place. Does it illuminate character? Does it build dramatic suspense? Does it show an important point of view? If a particular conversation doesn't accomplish a specific goal, consider whether the information could be better communicated through exposition.

What Events Make Good Scenes?

You can't make a scene out of every event in your life unless you want to create an awfully long book. Select events that lend themselves to a scene. Then use exposition to link the scenes together, to provide background information, to summarize an expanse of time. The following types of events provide good material for scenes:

• Humorous incidents

• Frightening situations

• Moments of crisis

• Events that illustrate personality

• Incidents associated with life-changing events such as birth, marriage, illness, death, starting a new job, enlisting in the military, moving to a new town, encountering a new acquaintance

• Anecdotes that add sparkle, interest, and understanding to your story

Scenes do not need to be long to serve their purpose. For example, you might notice potential in an expository sentence such as, "Grandpa always removed his working boots before he came in the back door for supper." It should be easy for you to expand on this by making some simple adjustments:

> Grandpa took off his working boots, then opened the back door and came into the kitchen. He plopped down at the head of the table and gave me a weary look. "What's for supper tonight, Junior?" he asked.
>
> Although we both knew the fare was bread and milk, I said, "Roast beef, mashed potatoes, and cherry pie," because I loved seeing his face break into a crinkly smile.

This short scene lets us into the lives of the boy and the old man and we find ourselves suddenly curious about their relationship and wondering why they always had bread and milk for supper. We begin to care.

The dialogue in your scenes should sound like natural speech, but stripped of the nonessential blathering that fills most conversations.

Transitions: Moving
between Scene and Exposition

Ideally your narrative will contain both scenes and exposition. How do you move back and forth between them without confusing your readers? Use transition words or sentences to communicate the shift. Notice below how a transition statement can be used to introduce the previous scene:

Introductory exposition

I lived with my grandfather throughout most of my childhood. We grew so close we had established routines that never varied, like our dinner menu.

Transition to a specific moment in time

One day I surprised him. (Narrowing the focus with the phrase *one day* prepares the reader for the brief scene that follows.)

Sometimes the opening sentence, in this case "Grandpa took off his working boots, then opened the back door," will clue the reader about the transition to a scene.

There are a number of phrases that help introduce a scene, phrases such as

- On one occasion …
- I'll never forget one incident …
- That reminds me of the time …
- For example …
- Then there was the time I …
- This is best illustrated by …

Include scenes in your personal history and you'll keep your readers with you to the end. Now it's time to practice.

Notes

    1. "Civil War," *Encyclopedia Americana,* International Edition (Danbury, Conn: Grolier, 1999), 6:798.

    2. Margaret Mitchell, *Gone with the Wind,* 60th Anniversary Edition (New York: Scribner, 1996), 360-61.

    3. Russell Baker, *Growing Up* (New York: Congden & Weed, 1982), 178.

Learn by Doing

6. Make a list of at least ten life-changing events (turning points) that influenced who you are today. Your list may include such events as a move to a new location, an achievement, a marriage, a crisis (illness, death, job loss, disaster, divorce), a chance remark from an acquaintance. For this assignment, list events that occurred at a specific time and place, such as the day you decided to get married, for instance, rather than things that happened over time, such as your growth as a person as you adapted to married life.

7. Choose a life-changing event from your list and develop it into a scene. Use dialogue that re-creates emotions you and others felt at that time. Try to avoid a scene with only "talking heads." Give your characters something to do when they speak so readers can visualize real people in a specific setting. For example, a mother could be drying dishes while she talks to her family. Perhaps she tosses the towel on the sink when someone says something that irritates her. Actions like these make scenes feel "real" because we can visualize what's transpiring.

8. Select an event in your life that did not have enormous significance in itself, but illustrates a particular character trait of yours or of another person in your life. Re-create the event as a scene. Use the principle of showing rather than telling so your reader can draw his or her own conclusions.

Chapter 4

Writing at the Gut Level

Let Your Feelings Show

*O*ne of our students, a retired Air Force pilot, wrote several touching stories about his courtship and subsequent marriage to his beloved Ann Marie. When he read these stories in class, he brought tears to the eyes of other students because he was not afraid to reveal his feelings in his writing.

On one occasion, however, he missed the mark. To gather details to write about his honeymoon at a charming old inn in Massachusetts, he consulted a brochure he had saved from his stay there years before. This seemed like a good idea in theory, and his story began nicely enough, with a description of the newlyweds driving up the tree-lined road to the inn. Then it became bogged down in endless details about the number of windows in the building, the style of furniture in the lobby, the size and depth of the nearby lake, etc.

The story turned out to be more about the inn than the honeymoon. It was important to include some details to establish the setting, of course; however, the author was writing the story primarily for his children. How interested would they be in what the inn looked like? We suspect they'd rather hear about their parents' feelings for each other at that important time in their lives. A diligent student, he returned the next week with a revised story that captured the romance that had been missing from his earlier draft.

Author William Zinsser said, "Fidelity to the facts is no free pass to the reader's attention."[1] Nor a pass, we could add, to the reader's *heart*. Your life story will be as interesting as your ability to express your feelings on paper. You've probably read a personal history written by someone who carefully described experiences he had during his life but never explained how these experiences affected him. In the end you may have felt you never got to know this person because he didn't reveal himself to you. It's difficult to empathize with writers who keep their feelings under wraps.

No doubt you've also read stories that stayed with you long after you closed the book. Maybe the characters were so well drawn you identified with them in some way. Maybe the plots were so vividly written that the author drew you into the story. Whatever the reason, the stories touched an emotional chord of some kind.

Surely, no one plans to write a sterile, colorless story that leaves the reader cold. But it happens all the time. Why?

Writing about feelings is difficult. It's more difficult for some than for others. There are plenty of people who fear appearing foolish or vulnerable if they share too much of themselves on paper. It's more comfortable, less risky, to stick to the facts. For instance, someone who has lost a spouse may feel more comfortable writing about the people who came to the funeral and about the food that was served afterward than telling how sad and frightened she felt about being abandoned. It's painful to write about such things. Many feel personal information like this should be kept private.

Should You Reveal Your Deep Dark Secrets?

How honestly should you write about yourself? It's a dilemma you'll encounter and have to resolve. Should you admit your insecurities and risk being judged weak? Should you state your opinions and risk being thought old-fashioned? Should you reveal past mistakes and risk losing the respect of your grandchildren? How much do readers really need to know about you?

"Fill your paper with the breathings of your heart."
—William Wordsworth

In the course of reading many personal histories, we've observed that the subjects of the stories become more believable, interesting, and likeable when they reveal their vulnerabilities, the traits that make them human. As you describe incidents in your life, explain how you felt about them. Don't be afraid to admit feelings of fear, guilt, jealousy, rage, or hurt.

In her memoir, *On Any Given Day,* Jessie Lee Brown Foveaux wrote about her troubled marriage to an abusive husband. Toward the end of the book, she said,

> If you have read this far, you will know that I could have done much better than I did. I told you earlier that your grandfather and his drinking buddies ruined my life. Now I know that wasn't true; I did that myself. I took a bushel of self pity along with a bushel of hate, added a large supply of false pride, and almost destroyed myself. No one can know how blind one can be better than I. I tremble when I think, What if I should have died?
>
> Well, I didn't and I remembered my grandpa

Jeff, my mama, and my daddy and the things they taught me. I started to try to change me. It took a long, long time. I had to talk to our Lord a lot and admit I had been so wrong to hate people. I had to ask forgiveness. It wasn't easy to look deep inside and take my share of the blame for the mess I was making of my life. As soon as I felt I was forgiven, it was much easier. The Lord helped me in so many ways.[2]

Do you think the author's family thought less of her because of this passage? It's unlikely. We think they probably sympathized with her and admired her for confessing to a typical human frailty.

When You're Too Close to the Event

Some people find comfort and healing by writing about emotional or traumatic events soon after they occur. Studies show that writing about these incidents reduces stress and prevents illnesses that sometimes follow in their wake. A number of students have enrolled in our classes to work through emotional experiences. Some have recently lost a family member, and they feel that writing about their loss will help them through the grieving process. Sometimes it does.

Some people, though, find it too difficult to describe their feelings about these events when they're so fresh in their minds. They need time to adjust to their situation and understand what has happened. If you fall into this category, we recommend you write about other experiences and come back to the difficult stories after more time has passed.

How to Write from the "Gut Level"

Let's look at the different ways you can write about an incident typically charged with strong feelings—the day you became engaged. You could write, "John proposed to me in my home on June 10, 1965."

Not good. No feelings there.

How about this? "When John proposed on June 10, 1965, it was one of the most thrilling days of my life."

Okay, there's an inkling of emotion. But how thrilling was it?

It requires more skill to make your readers *feel* the same emotion you experienced when John proposed to you. You'll agree that the following example better accomplishes this purpose.

> After dinner, John and I went into the living room to talk. I sat on the sofa expecting him to join me, but he just stood there in the middle of the rug staring at me. He looked like he wanted to say something, like he was about to give a speech. It suddenly occurred to me that he was going to propose. Yes, that was it! My heart started pumping in wild bursts. I felt like I couldn't breathe.
>
> When he reached into the pocket of his suit, I stood up and started walking toward him, wanting to soothe his awkwardness, reduce the tension of the moment. I took a few steps and suddenly felt lightheaded. I couldn't see him in front of me anymore.
>
> The next thing I knew, I was lying on the floor, my head in John's lap. He looked worried. Then he grinned and said, "I've fallen for you, too, Julie. You have to marry me."

This scene dramatizes the couple's feelings. We see how Julie and John physically and emotionally respond to the

"Don't tell me the moon is shining. Show me the glint of light on broken glass."
— Anton Chekhov

stress of the moment. We learn that they love each other, that John is awkward, that Julie wants to save him from discomfort. So not only do we understand their feelings, we learn a little about their personalities. A one-sentence summary of this significant event doesn't do it justice.

Writing Techniques That Help Convey Feelings

1. Describe how your body reacts to emotions.

How does your body react to fright, pleasure, disappointment? Learn how to describe those reactions rather than just reporting that you *felt* such an emotion ("I was so happy").

A word of caution … When describing feelings, many beginners have a tendency to rely on cliché descriptions. Even though people react in similar ways when they are emotionally stimulated, if their reactions are always described the same way, they lose their power on the page. Here are examples of the sort of tired phrases you should avoid:

- My legs were weak with fear.

- My heart pounded with excitement.

- I tingled in anticipation.

- My mouth felt like cotton when I rose to speak.

- I was blind with rage.

- I was delirious with happiness.

It takes some creativity to come up with fresh ways to describe feelings. Next time you read a novel, notice how the author handles this task. In the meantime, here are a few creative examples we found:

- Her body, as if it belonged to someone else, began to

shake with a dry, sharp rack she was helpless to stop, a strange weeping from her throat that sounded almost like laughter.[3]

• I bounce my feet around a little, but I can feel Steve's eyes. I look his way, just to make sure. Steve smiles a little bit of a smile and I look away again, prickles up the back of my neck, over the top of my head, down into my nose.[4]

• Daily life was in black and white, like a badly made film. My trancelike state excluded music, feeling, color, desire.[5]

2. Show how feelings translate into behavior.

Feelings usually manifest themselves in actions. To write compellingly, you need to describe the behavior that results from the emotion. Instead of writing, "Mom went through a period of depression after my father died," explain how she slept more than usual, failed to return phone calls, paid little attention to her appearance. This will resonate with readers far more than if you simply say she was depressed.

Here's an example from Lisa See's family history, *On*

Learn by Doing

9. Notice how your body reacts the next time you feel a strong emotion. Write down these reactions for future use. Note how other people display emotions. What happens to their faces and their voices? What do they do with their hands? What other kinds of body language do they display? Record your observations.

10. Think of a time you were frightened. What kind of behavior did you display? What did you say? Describe the incident and your reaction to it. Try to be as honest and specific as you can. Let readers feel your fear.

Gold Mountain, illustrating how the author's great-grandmother felt after the end of her marriage:

> Her anger at him had long burned out, to be replaced by grief, then a final, horrible emptiness. She was a ghost of herself. She went through the motions of conducting business, but she pushed Ming to take on more responsibility. She did her duty as a mother, knowing that none of her children really needed her anymore. She acted the part of a good friend, but she could be in a roomful of people and feel the deepest loneliness.[6]

Notice how the author convinces us of the intensity of the woman's sense of abandonment, illustrating it through the woman's behavior rather than by simply telling us she felt bereft.

In another example from Frank McCourt's *Angela's Ashes,* young McCourt learns a former girlfriend has died. The author had a physically intimate relationship with her and had been feeling guilty about it prior to hearing about her death. The selection below describes the behavior that arose out of his tumultuous feelings of grief, remorse, and fear:

> I slip the telegram under the door and cycle back down to the Franciscan church to beg for the repose of Theresa's soul. I pray to every statue, to the stained glass windows, the Stations of the Cross. I swear I'll lead a life of faith, hope and charity, poverty, chastity and obedience.
>
> Next day, I go to four Masses, I do the Stations of the Cross three times, I say rosaries all day. I go without food and drink and wherever I find a quiet place I cry....[7]

Read one of these published memoirs to learn how to incorporate feelings into your writing.

• Maya Angelou: *I Know Why the Caged Bird Sings*

• Rick Bragg: *All Over but the Shoutin'* and *Ava's Man*

• Mary Karr: *The Liar's Club*

• Jennifer Lauck: *Blackbird: A Childhood Lost and Found*

• Frank McCourt: *Angela's Ashes* and *'Tis*

• Tobias Woolf: *This Boy's Life*

McCourt's writing technique illuminates his state of mind on learning of his friend's death. He strings together in one sentence several actions—praying to every statue, to the stained glass windows, to the Stations of the Cross. In the next sentence, he swears he'll live a life committed to six different virtues. The excessiveness of McCourt's behavior (emphasized by the long sentences), helps us visualize the depth of his conscience-stricken desperation.

3. Dramatize the emotion of the moment.

There's no more effective way to convey how you felt at a particular time than to capture the moment as a scene. Visual impressions and actions communicate far more emotion than flat summary sentences like, "I was furious the time my sister left the gate open and my dog ran away." In a scene, you can demonstrate anger with yelling, name-calling, slamming doors.

In *Growing Up*, Russell Baker dramatizes the anger of his stepfather after being awakened by a prank phone call, the caller identifying himself as Benito Mussolini:

> It was one of the few times I saw Herb in a violent mood. He stormed out of the bedroom with a racket that woke me in my bedroom across the hall, and I stumbled out to investigate. Herb was standing in the hallway roaring, "Mussolini! Mussolini, my foot!" Herb never cursed; "my foot!" was the strongest oath in his vocabulary.
>
> He was belting up his trousers for an assault on the landlord, whom he suspected of being the prankster since the landlord was Lithuanian and "Mussolini" had spoken in a Lithuanian accent. My mother calmed him by pointing out that the

landlord didn't have a telephone, so couldn't possibly have made the offending call. Herb pondered the logic of that for a moment, then let his rage dissolve into a grin. He wasn't a man for smashing furniture when he was angry. "Mussolini," he said to himself, shaking his head as if it had been a great joke after all. Then, loosening his belt and heading for the mattress: "I've got to get my rest."[8]

The above example not only portrays emotions, it has all the ingredients of a good scene—a feel for characters, a sense of the relationships between people, a glimpse into the times in which the incident occurred.

The following excerpt from Maya Angelou's *I Know Why the Caged Bird Sings* grabs the reader's emotions by vividly revealing the feelings of everyone involved in the scene:

> There was no chance to warn Bailey that he was dangerously late, that everybody had been worried and that he should create a good lie, or, better, a great one.
>
> Momma said, "Bailey, Junior," and he looked up without surprise. "You know it's night and you just now getting home?"
>
> "Yes, ma'am." He was empty. Where was his alibi?
>
> "What you been doing?"
>
> "Nothing."
>
> "That's all you got to say?"
>
> "Yes, ma'am."
>
> "All right, young man. We'll see when you get home."
>
> She had turned me loose, so I made a grab for

Bailey's hand, but he snatched it away. I said, "Hey, Bail," hoping to remind him that I was his sister and his only friend, but he grumbled something like, "Leave me alone."

Momma didn't turn on the flashlight on the way back, nor did she answer the questioning Good evenings that floated around us as we passed the darkened houses.

I was confused and frightened. He was going to get a whipping and maybe he had done something terrible. If he couldn't talk to me it must have been serious. But there was no air of spent revelry about him. He just seemed sad, and I didn't know what to think.[9]

Your life story will resonate more with your readers if you learn to write at the gut level. Don't keep your readers at a distance. Ask yourself, would it be so bad for people to know this about me? What would including this information add to the story? If left out, what would be missed? Experiment writing the same material in different ways and ask someone you trust to tell you which version increases her understanding of you.

Learn by Doing

11. Pick an incident in your life when you felt an intense emotion and dramatize that event in a scene. Be honest. Feel the emotion when you're writing. Pour everything out onto the paper in your first draft, then go back and polish it.

12. Read a chapter or two from a novel or one of the memoirs listed in Chapter 1. Notice, in particular, examples that illustrate how the characters reveal their feelings.

Notes

1. William Zinsser, *Inventing the Truth: The Art and Craft of Memoir* (New York: Houghton Mifflin, 1987), 25.

2. Jessie Lee Brown Foveaux, *On Any Given Day* (New York: Warner Books, 1997), 251.

3. Barbara Kingsolver, *Prodigal Summer* (New York: HarperCollins, 2000), 71.

4. Jennifer Lauck, *Blackbird: A Childhood Lost and Found* (New York: Simon & Schuster, 2000), 113.

5. Jill Ker Conway, *The Road from Coorain* (New York: Vintage, 1989), 121.

6. Lisa See, *On Gold Mountain* (New York: St. Martin's Press, 1995), 174-75.

7. McCourt, *Angela's Ashes,* 325.

8. Baker, *Growing Up,* 226.

9. Maya Angelou, *I Know Why the Caged Bird Sings* (New York: Bantam, 1993), 97.

:· MY FAMILY TREE ·:

Chapter 5

Writing about People
Breathe Life into Your "Characters"

*S*oon after you begin writing your personal history, you'll discover that your story is also about relatives, friends, teachers, employers, mentors, religious figures, boyfriends, girlfriends, rivals—people who have played a role in your life and probably influenced to some extent who you are. You can't tell your story without them.

Most of these individuals should be more than mere names on your pages. Your readers need to know something about their appearance, their personalities, their behavior, and their influence on you. In other words, your task as a writer is to bring them to life so readers can see them as you do. This may sound like a lot of work, but it will make all the difference in your writing. If your people appear flat and lifeless, your story will too.

Unless you have a background in fiction writing, you've probably had little practice with what novelists and screen writers call "character development." Non-fiction writers can benefit from studying how good novelists bring their characters to life. Their techniques can be used with great effect in personal histories.

Let's consider, for a moment, some memorable characters from fiction. Mark Twain's Huckleberry Finn, Charles Dickens' Ebenezer Scrooge, and Jane Austen's Elizabeth Bennet are three figures most people can identify. These protagonists are so well drawn, they seem like real people. Why? Because their creators have captured their unique traits and physical attributes. These characters have strengths, they have flaws, they have a quirky individuality that makes them who they are.

You can make the people in your own story seem similarly alive. If you're like most of our students, you're saying: "I'm no Twain or Dickens or Austen. They had special gifts. And besides, they're working with fictional characters, so they can make them as interesting as they want them to be. I'm writing about real people. I have to work with what I have."

This is true, to a degree. Nevertheless, you will be surprised how much more readable you can make your story by utilizing some learnable techniques that add flesh to your characters.

We're not suggesting you become so fanciful in your descriptions you transform dull Uncle Stanley into a charming rascal to make your life story more interesting. But your uncle has to be more than just *Stanley* to your readers. Develop his dullness. Show readers Stanley's hypochondria, his addiction to television infomercials. Show us *dull*.

This chapter will teach you how.

Keep It Real

A story rings true when we recognize its similarity to our own experiences. It's crucial that the people in your story be realistically drawn so they feel true to life. When your family reads about their Grandma Gunderson, they should think, *That's Grandma in a nutshell.* Others who may not know her should see something in Grandma that is similar to what they've experienced with their own grandmothers or at least is recognizable as being in the realm of human nature.

Characters come to life when they seem human, which means, among other things, they have imperfections. You have to show all sides of people—their strengths and their weaknesses. This can be one of the most difficult aspects of writing your personal history, particularly if you're writing about people who are still living.

Realism goes hand in hand with honesty. If you portray your characters candidly, you come closer to capturing the whole person. Saints come across as stick figures. You've likely read about some of these paragons of virtue in family histories written by well-meaning relatives. These sorts of histories are tedious to read because the people in them are so one-dimensional no one can relate to them.

By stressing honesty and realism as components of good character development, we are not advocating you write the next *Mommy Dearest*! Stories that whine, blame, and seek revenge are as boorish as those that cast a rosy glow over everyone and everything. As the author, you are the custodian of the reputations of the people in your story. It's one thing to tell someone a secret; it's another to commit that secret to paper and publish it for everyone to see. Writing about peo-

People appear realistic when they seem human, which means they have imperfections.

ple is a heavy responsibility, requiring a thoughtful balancing act. You're juggling a desire to write the truth as you understand it with the feelings of friends and relatives who may appear in your pages. You may feel you're walking a tightrope, trying to maintain your integrity as a writer while trying to remain on good terms with the people around you. It's a problem our students struggle with as much as anything, and unfortunately there are no easy answers. Each writer has to come to a solution she can live with.

Some authors seem to manage this balancing act well. Their stories have the ring of truth—truth told with love, respect, and sometimes with a dash of humor. In Tobias Wolff's *This Boy's Life,* the author writes about being trapped in a childhood governed by an abusive stepfather and a loving but bungling mother. Wolff doesn't carp or whimper or censure. Instead, he tells his story with honesty, grace, and forgiveness. He helps us understand the essential humanity of the imperfect people in his life, and he reveals his own foibles with the same candor and acceptance.

Wolff establishes this tone in the opening scene. The author, on the cusp of adolescence, and his mother are fleeing an unhappy home. As they chug along a mountain road in their rattletrap Nash Rambler, a truck screeches around them, horn blaring, brakes gone. Further down the road, the Wolffs come upon the devastation: The truck has plunged off a cliff into the ravine below. The mother, shaken and reminded of life's fragility, turns to her son protectively. Her son reports in his memoir,

> For the rest of the day she kept looking over at me, touching me, brushing back my hair. I saw that the time was right to make a play for souvenirs. I

knew she had no money for them, and I had tried not to ask, but now that her guard was down I couldn't help myself. When we pulled out of Grand Junction I owned a beaded Indian belt, beaded moccasins, and a bronze horse with a removable, tooled saddle.[1]

Wolff's wry description of himself feels true. Children can be selfish and manipulative, and Wolff is not afraid to acknowledge his own craftiness. Because he is so forthright, we sense he is a narrator we can trust.

Capture the "Look" of the People in Your Story

Readers need to have a mental picture of your characters, and not in a vague way ("Dad was of average height and build"), but through details that show the uniqueness of their appearance. Caricaturists make careers out of capturing the prominent physical characteristics of politicians and celebrities in simple sketches. They draw actor Bob Hope with a ski-jump nose. They show George Burns with a cigar. They emphasize Richard Nixon's five-o'clock shadow. When we see a caricature, we recognize the subject in an instant, even though it's not a literal portrayal.

Likewise, your descriptions of your characters' physical appearances should capture their unique "look"—the physical qualities that make them who they are. Sometimes we get so used to people after years of association with them, we forget what they look like. Nearly everyone has something about his or her appearance that stands out. Try to remember what you noticed about your subjects the first time you saw them. How would you describe them to a stranger? Look at a photo if you have trouble remembering and jot down a few notes about what you see.

Consider your mother, for example. What is unique about her appearance? Does she have any prominent facial features? Is there something memorable about her hairstyle? What about the way she dresses? What styles and colors does she prefer? How would you describe her height and build? What would strangers recall after meeting her?

Be precise. Steer away from vague, general descriptions. Explaining that your mother is short, attractive, and a stylish dresser may mean something to you, but the portrayal is too broad to be meaningful to others. How do you define short? Dawn's mother is five feet tall, short for our times, but close to average for women of her generation. Words like *attractive* and *good looking* are also too general and subjective to be meaningful. And if you are of a mature generation, your conception of a stylish dresser probably differs from that of most young people today.

In other words, be specific. Choose words that identify exactly what you mean. Don't always be satisfied with the first word or phrase that comes to mind. For example, there are many ways to convey someone's attractiveness more precisely than merely saying he or she is "handsome" or "pretty." Consider alternatives such as these:

- People always said Mother reminded them of the movie star Lana Turner, that sultry blond beauty popular in the forties and fifties.

- She turned heads wherever she went.

- When she smiled, her face lit up like a child's at an amusement park.

- Her raven hair, creamy complexion, and lustrous blue eyes reminded others of a magazine "cover girl."

Steer away from vague, general descriptions. Be specific, choosing words that identify exactly what you mean.

These examples create a clearer image of attractiveness, don't they? They grab the reader's attention more than general terms like "nice looking." Notice how it's done:

• They compare someone to another person known for her distinctive beauty.

• They show how a person's appearance affects the people around them.

• They specify certain features that help readers visualize what sort of attractiveness the character possesses.

The following example from Vivian Gornick's *Fierce Attachments* uses all three methods to describe Nettie Levine, as seen through the eyes of a twelve-year-old girl:

> I bent, blushing, to help her retrieve the bags scattered across the landing and saw that she had bright red hair piled high on her head in a pompadour and streaming down her back and over her shoulders. Her features were narrow and pointed (the eyes almond-shaped, the mouth and nose thin and sharp), and her shoulders were wide but she was slim. She reminded me of the pictures of Greta Garbo. My heart began to pound. I had never before seen a beautiful woman.[2]

Nettie comes alive because of Gornick's specific physical details. Can you visualize Nettie's hair? When describing people in your life, remember that hair colors come in all shades and that hairstyles come in all varieties. Define the color. Turn someone's "short blond hair" into something we can visualize, like a "platinum pageboy" or a "tawny crewcut" or a "sandy duck tail."

Think of all the shades of yellow. Was your high school prom dress the color of daffodils, mustard, wheat fields, butter, or sunshine? J. I. Rodale's *The Synonym Finder*,[3] a handy resource for your writing library, lists thirty-eight alternatives to plain old yellow. Are your sister's eyes a true green or are they hazel? What about that blue dress your mother wore on her fiftieth anniversary? Was it turquoise, peacock blue, or navy? Be specific.

Your descriptions of people should also offer a clear picture of their attire. "He always dressed in a casual shirt and pants" can be enlivened by instead having him wear a khaki work shirt, an Oxford button-down with rolled-up sleeves, or a paisley knit pullover. His pants could be faded jeans, worn khakis, pleated gabardines, or any number of styles that would call forth a more vivid image than mere *pants*.

Evaluate your word choices with a critical eye, particularly your selection of nouns, verbs, and adjectives. Consult a good thesaurus for other words to consider.

Browse through Memoirs and Novels for Ideas

As you read best-selling memoirs, notice how the authors write about people. In most cases, you'll find these people interesting and well developed. Underline memorable words and phrases. Notice the author's style. Does the author describe a character's appearance when he or she is first introduced or is it revealed piecemeal throughout a chapter? How specific is the description? Can you visualize the people? Do they seem "real"?

Pulitzer Prize-winning author Russell Baker writes masterful physical description. Note his attention to specific detail in his portrayal of his Uncle Lewis in *Growing Up*.

Uncle Lewis was my first vision of what male

"A good storyteller is a person with a good memory and hopes other people haven't."
—George Bernard Shaw

elegance could be. He had glistening black hair always parted so meticulously that you might have thought he needed surveyor's instruments to comb a line so straight. Thin black sideburns extended down to his earlobes in the style cartoonists adopted as the distinguishing mark of high-toned cads. With a high gloss on his city shoes, in his crisp white barber's smock, he wisecracked with the railroad men as he presided in front of a long wall of mirrors lined with pomades, tonics, and scents. I admired him as the ultimate in dandyism.[4]

Baker uses precise and colorful language. Uncle Lewis doesn't just have dark hair with sideburns; he has glistening black hair with long thin sideburns. He doesn't just wear shoes; he wears city shoes polished to a high gloss. His hair doesn't merely have a part; it's a part so precise Baker wonders if surveyors' instruments were used.

Placing Uncle Lewis in front of the mirror and the assortment of pomades and tonics accentuates the man's fastidiousness, a trait that was obviously impressive to country boy Baker. The uncle *wisecracks* and *presides,* terms that suggest his self-confidence and ease with people.

But Baker isn't paying homage here. Notice the use of words with negative connotations—*high-toned cads and dandyism*—to suggest that Uncle Lewis may have possessed an underlying shallowness the younger Baker unconsciously recognized, even in the midst of his hero worship.

Use All the Senses

In Jennifer Lauck's memoir, *Blackbird: A Childhood Lost and Found,* the narrator is a sensitive, kindergarten-age girl who is wise and observant beyond her years. As the constant caretaker of her chronically ill mother, she misses nothing about the people around her:

> Aunt Georgia is thin, thin, bird thin, and she wears navy blue shorts and a blue and white striped tank top. Momma says Aunt Georgia dresses sportswear mix-and-match.
>
> "I need more than a wave, little girl," Aunt Georgia says. "Come give me a hug."
>
> Momma laughs and Aunt Georgia puts her tanned arms wide. Aunt Georgia always gives me a hug when she comes to visit and I like that about her, like how she smells like soap and toothpaste and the same kind of almond lotion that Momma uses.[5]

Notice how the sense of smell adds to our conception of Aunt Georgia. The author uses the same technique a few pages later when she introduces her father:

> Daddy settles me against his chest and I fit just right in the crook of his arm. This close he smells like tobacco and coffee and That Man cologne and I can see how his eyes are lots of different colors of brown, like spices all ground up.[6]

When you describe people, don't just write about what you see: their physical appearance. Your memories of them likely involve associations with certain fragrances—cologne, soap, tobacco—or smells related to occupation—turpentine, chalk, farm animals. Write with your nose, your ears, and your fingers, not just with your eyes. Capture on paper Cousin Jim's knuckle cracking, Aunt Betsy's soup slurping, or Grandpa Walker's wheezing. What about the velvety softness of your baby's skin or the splotchy roughness of your

Write with your nose, your ears, and your fingers, not just with your eyes.

piano teacher's hands? Noting little peculiarities like these helps individualize your characters so your readers can visualize them.

A Word of Caution

Bringing people to life on your pages is no easy feat because humans are complex and baffling. There's so much you could say about these people. However, you are not writing *their* biography. This is *your* story. Don't overwhelm us with so much information you bog down your storyline. Choose details that show off a character's uniqueness and demonstrate what made him or her memorable for you. This takes planning and practice.

"Why would anybody lie? The truth is always more colourful."
—Jerry Hall

Capture Behavior Traits and Mannerisms

We all draw conclusions about people by observing their behavior, often making vague assumptions like:

Aunt Mavis has a good heart.

My brother has a hidden tender streak.

The widow next door is a real fussbudget.

Grandpa Evans has a nervous disposition.

These are general, summary statements that label a person based on observed behavior, but they do little to paint a picture of what these people are really like. Your reader can't visualize someone with a "good heart" unless he is shown examples of behavior that caused you to use that description.

As you write your story, create indelible images by describing behavior and letting your readers draw their own conclusions. For example, instead of writing, "My mother was kind and generous to strangers" (a summary statement), explain in what way she was kind and generous. You might say, "I don't remember my mother ever turning away a beggar without giving him a few dollars." Now we begin to understand what this woman was like.

Here are some more examples:

Summary statement	My mother was frugal.
Illustrative behavior	My mother never put more than two inches of water in the sink when washing dishes.
Summary statement	Dad was an impatient man.
Illustrative behavior	Dad often finished sentences for me when I tried to tell him something.
Summary statement	Edith had a quirky sense of humor.
Illustrative behavior	Edith kept them laughing at the Senior Center by wearing outlandish hats to their monthly meetings. She must have owned a hundred crazy hats.

The illustrations describing behavior help create a more vivid image in the reader's mind. This may seem fairly rudimentary, but in practice it's easy to forget. You'd be surprised how often our students describe people who have played important roles in their lives with the broadest kinds of generalities. They want their readers to know these people, yet their bland descriptions have sucked the life out of them.

Everyone has certain unique mannerisms and behavior traits. Before you begin to write, consider making a list of all the little things you recall your characters "doing." For instance, does she always chew gum? Does he clear his throat before he begins to speak? Does she fold her arms across her chest when talking to other people? Does he play with his hair or stroke his mustache or eyebrows? Does she bite her nails or crack her knuckles? Is he always checking his watch, cleaning his glasses, straightening his tie?

These "quirks" of behavior make people who they are. Generally we find them endearing, but they can also be annoying. In any case, including them will make your characters—and your story—more memorable.

In the example below from Vivian Gornick's *Fierce Attachments,* the author translates character traits into actions we can visualize. Notice how she captures the eccentricities of her neighbor, Mrs. Kerner, by simply describing how she cleans her house:

> She was a terrible housekeeper who never stopped keeping house. At all times she had a rag tied around her head, a feather duster in her hand, and an expression of confusion in her eyes. She would wander around the house, aimlessly flicking the duster here and there. Or, she'd drag out an iron monster of a vacuum cleaner, start it up with a terrific whining noise that made you think a plane was about to land in the living room, push it across

the threadbare carpet a few times, lose interest, and leave the vacuum cleaner standing where she turned it off, sometimes for two or three days.[7]

Mrs. Kerner seems like a real person here, someone we know, because Gornick carefully captures the idiosyncrasies of her behavior and appearance. It's the quirks that make us unique. If you bring these out in your characters, your story will spring to life.

Show How People Have Affected You

We all grew up surrounded by people who inspired us, irritated us, cheered and depressed us. We can't be around others without feeling some kind of reaction to them. Enliven your story by describing those reactions. Consider the following examples:

- Dad's frown made me break into a sweat.

- My piano teacher was so pretty I dressed more carefully on lesson day than I did any other time in the week.

- I felt like such a country bumpkin whenever I was around my older sister.

Descriptions such as these serve a dual purpose in your memoir because they convey information not only about the person you are describing, but also about you. In an excerpt from "Into the Woods," author Bill Roorbach offers a glimpse into his relationship with his employer. At the same time, we also learn a great deal about how Roorbach feels about his father.

> Working beside him (tradesmen often touch—four hands to pull the cable, four arms reaching into a small space, heads together to look into a ser-

vice panel … hey, hold my legs while I lean out over this here abyss), I'd feel sometimes like I was with my dad. It was Larry's thin hair, maybe, or the Aqua Velva and cigarettes, or just regular old transference. I spent every day beside this parallel-universe effigy of my father, and I was mad at Larry almost always and desperate to impress him.

One day he said I had good hands, and that little compliment was everything—I glowed, I crowed, I told my friends, my folks. I stared at my hands late at night in bars, stared at them for hours, entranced.[8]

If you've read our chapter carefully, you noticed Roorbach's attention to detail—his vivid description of his work activities, the particulars about Larry's and his father's similar appearance, and the revelations about how the author felt about both of them. This is good character development.

How did the people in your life affect you? Were you excited to see your parents? Did you feel dread when you heard your brother's voice on the phone? Did your feelings about certain people change over time? Including this infor-

Learn by Doing

14. Choose someone you know well. Write a sentence that summarizes one of his or her dominant personality traits, a sentence as simple as, "My sister was a non-stop talker." Now make a list of examples demonstrating the trait. Finally, write a paragraph using these examples. Does he or she come alive on the page?

15. Write about a "crush" you had on someone during your adolescence. Be honest and specific about your feelings. Were you embarrassed? Angry? Shy? Jubilant? Carefully describe his or her appearance, personality, and behavior. What is it about that person that especially attracted you?

mation is an important way to let your readers know these people—and you. At first it may seem you're exposing yourself more than you want to, admitting feelings you'd rather keep hidden, but your openness will mean the difference between a life story that feels distant and sterile and one that genuinely moves the reader.

Put Your People in a Scene

In Chapter 3 we discussed the importance of including scenes in your story. There is no more effective way to make your people come alive than to put them in a scene so they can speak and interact with others. A scene lets readers see your characters in action. Let's say you want to explain that your parents had a penchant for risky adventures. You could convey this information with a vague description, as follows:

> My parents were unconventional, to put it mildly. They were always involved in some zany scheme that pushed the boundaries of acceptable behavior in our community. We kids found their shenanigans exciting and scary at the same time.

A better strategy would be to mention a specific example to help the reader visualize what you mean by "unconventional" and "zany schemes." How about this for starters:

> I still get goose bumps when I recall the night Dad dug up plants in the neighbor's yard because Mom wanted some "free plants." I watched the whole thing from my bedroom window, my heart racing with fear and excitement. When I heard the sirens go off, I thought this time Dad would be hauled off to the slammer for sure.

Ok, now we get the picture more clearly through the drama portrayed here. The details of this escapade enlighten us regarding these people. Still, Dad and Mom haven't really come alive yet to the extent that we feel like we're there beside them. Let's re-create this incident as a scene, as one of our students did for a class assignment.

Flashing Lights in the Night

It was a wet, heavy fog. A person could only move about in the neighborhood if he knew the area well—and he knew the area well, very well! He had been "casing" the house for over a week now. He raised his hand in front of his eyes. Yes! He could barely see it, so-o-o tonight was the night to strike.

Quietly, he approached the side of the house, pleased to see that the windows were dark. Stooping down, he peered intently at the plants in the flowerbed, looking for the ones he had decided on earlier. Carefully he placed the edge of the shovel he carried into the dirt near a medium-sized clump of growth. Nervously, he glanced to see if the windows were still dark and listened for the sounds of approaching footsteps. All clear so far.

He gently pressed the shovel down into the dirt with one foot. The soft crunch as the shovel entered the earth sounded deafening and he was sure everyone in the neighborhood heard him and were coming to investigate. NOTHING! Breathing a silent sigh of relief and lifting slowly, he freed the plant from the damp earth. Success!

Suddenly, sirens blared. Lights flashed behind him, casting a red glow to the haze of fog. Metal doors clanked closed.

Startled and frightened, he fell into the flowerbed. He could feel the dampness of sweat in his armpits, and his heart was beating frantically.

Lying there among the bushes and flowers, he realized what was happening. The neighborhood fire station behind him across Third Street had come to life in response to a fire alarm.

Slowly he pushed himself up off the ground, brushed himself off, picked up the shovel and pilfered flowers, and limped home through the fog. Once home, he informed his wife, my mother, "You want anything else stolen, you'll steal it yourself."

Thus ended Jim Blaine's only attempt to acquire "free" plants.[9]

This scene puts us in the moment so that we're right there with Jim Blaine, seeing the fog, sharing the risk, hearing the sirens, feeling the danger. The scene is more effective —and interesting—than the previous two examples. Practice revealing your characters' personalities through scenes, as our student did in this story.

Learn by Doing

16. Pick an incident from your life that illustrates the personality of someone close to you and re-create that incident in a scene. Try to reconstruct the conversation that occurred. Describe where the incident took place so your readers can visualize the setting.

17. Choose a person who played an important role in your life and write a physical description of that person using specific details that show her prominent traits. Use more than one sensory clue if you can. What fragrances was this person known for? Is there something notable about the way she talks? Write a quick first draft, then examine your writing, evaluating words and phrases, adding, substituting, deleting, moving phrases around to create different effects.

Scenes Let Your Characters Speak

Most scenes involve conversations. By letting your characters speak, you reveal something about their personalities, their speech patterns, and their point of view. In the following example, another from Russell Baker's *Growing Up,* his widowed mother asks her brother, Uncle Jack, to take Russell upstairs and explain "the facts of life." The conversation between uncle and nephew is strained and brief, but we learn a great deal about each of them, both from *what* is said and *how* it is said.

When you let your characters speak, you give them life.

> We were slowly exhausting baseball. Uncle Jack went back to the window and looked out again, then turned to face me.
>
> "Look here," he said, "you know how babies are made, don't you?"
>
> "Sure," I said.
>
> "Well that's all there is to it," he said.
>
> "I know that," I said.
>
> "I thought you did," he said.
>
> "Sure," I said.
>
> "Let's go back downstairs," he said.
>
> We went downstairs together.
>
> "Did you tell him?" my mother asked.
>
> "Everything," Uncle Jack said.[10]

Through this amusing interchange, Baker tells us far more about his uncle's personality than had he merely summarized the incident.

In Chapter 3 we discussed how to re-create conversations from our past. If you're feeling hesitant about making up dialogue, refer back to that chapter for a review of the pros and cons, along with our recommendations.

Can you illustrate the personality traits of the major characters in your life with a vivid scene? Try it by doing the exercises on the next page.

Metaphors Create Vivid Images

Simply put, metaphors are a literary device that make a point by comparing one thing to another. Shakespeare used a metaphor when he wrote, "All the world's a stage." Had Shakespeare written, "All the world is like a stage" (or *as* a stage), he would have used the related device known as a simile, which uses the words *like* and *as* to make a comparison. If your similes and metaphors are apt and clever, you can clarify in a few words, with a strong visual picture, what may have taken a whole paragraph to explain.

Notice how the following examples create memorable images:

- "She kept on and on like a fugue, demanding that I agree with her that her actions had been warranted."[11]

- "My fine, black hair was straight as a kite string on a windy day."[12]

- "[H]is pockets were as empty as a banker's soul."[13]

- "My momma inherited his love of stories, but not his timing, so that when she talks about him, the words come out in a jumbled rush, like puppies spilling out of a cardboard box, jumping all over each other."[14]

Try to create figures of speech that are fresh and clever. Avoid hackneyed expressions (cool as a cucumber, strong as an ox, red as a beet), that were fresh at one time but have become clichés.

As we said at the beginning, your story will come alive to the extent that you make your people come alive. The examples in this chapter illustrate techniques typically used by fiction writers to create believable and memorable characters. Some were written by professionals who have spent a lifetime developing their skills. Don't let their gift for description discourage you. Learn from them. Analyze what works and why it works. Try applying some of their methods to your writing. Be patient with yourself as you expand your skills. In time, you'll also be able to bring your "characters" to life on the page so your readers will know them as you do.

"A writer begins by breathing life into his characters. But if you are very lucky, they breathe life into you."
—Caryl Phillips

Learn by Doing

18. Choose three individuals who will be main characters in your life story. Compose a metaphor or simile to describe a personality trait of each of these characters. (Example: My brother was as lazy as a kite on a windless day.) Try to create a comparison that conveys a vivid image of that trait.

Notes

1. Tobias Wolff, *This Boy's Life* (New York: Grove Press, 1989), 4.

2. Vivian Gornick, *Fierce Attachments* (Boston: Beacon Press, 1987), 34.

3. J. I Rodale, *The Synonym Finder* (New York: Warner Books, 1978).

4. Baker, *Growing Up*, 69.

5. Lauck, *Blackbird,* 13.

6. Ibid., 20-21.

7. Gornick, *Fierce Attachments,* 27.

8. Bill Roorbach, "Into the Woods," in *Writing Life Stories* by Bill Roorbach (Cincinnati: Story Press, 1998), 194.

9. Clara Jo McLenahan, "Flashing Lights in the Night," 2001.

10. Baker, *Growing Up,* 168.

11. Conway, *Road from Coorain,* 231.

12. Ruth McQuerry, *Blossoming in the Show Me State* (Brea, Calif.: Creative Continuum, 2004), 100.

13. Conway, *Road from Coorain,* 29.

14. Rick Bragg, *All Over but the Shoutin'* (New York: Pantheon, 1997), 28.

Chapter 6

Writing about Places

Put Your Life on the Map

*M*any years ago, when we were in college, we attended a production of Samuel Beckett's *Waiting for Godot,* a play attracting wide interest at the time. We heard it was an avant-garde play. We didn't know exactly what that meant but decided to take a chance. We walked into the theater and found the stage empty except for a couple of folding metal chairs and a scrawny fake tree. Green as we were about such things, we found the lack of setting disorienting at first. We missed all those "scenery cues" that ground the plot in a specific place and time. The producers had created the spare set design for effect, of course, to focus the attention of the audience on what they saw as the play's universal message, but we still missed all the trappings of a traditional set.

What does *Waiting for Godot* have to do with writing about your life? Simply this: Don't write an avant-garde-style personal history. Many do when they write statements like, "I was born in Pittston, Pennsylvania, in 1933," and then fail to describe what Pittston was like at that time. If you don't provide enough setting cues, your readers will miss a substantial part of what your life was all about.

Dawn, for example, grew up in Orange County, California, at a time when Disneyland was in its infancy, communities were small and insular, and orange groves still blanketed a significant part of the area. If in her life story she failed to describe Orange County as it was in "her day," some of her readers would envision a childhood spent amid the freeways, fast food restaurants, amusement parks, and expensive real estate for which the county is noted today.

Let Your Hayseed Show

We're all products of our environment, whether we like it or not. Your hometown probably influenced the kinds of hobbies you pursued, the style of clothes you wore, the principles that guided your life, the way your parents disciplined you, the image you had of yourself. Your school and career choices may have been shaped by your environment as well. Would your life have been different had you lived somewhere else? For most of us, the answer would likely be yes. It's important, then, that you consider how to bring your readers into the times and places that have formed your life. Otherwise, your experiences will seem to have occurred against a blank backdrop.

Personalizing Your Environment

Sometimes we become so used to a particular location, we forget what's unique about it. What would a visitor from a different part of the country notice about your town? Bring out all the details that will personalize it for your readers.

Here are some topics to consider when trying to recall and describe the town where you grew up:

- **Geography and terrain**. Was it mountainous, flat, hilly, covered with brush, lush trees? What was the water source? Did the geography play a role in your leisure activities?

- **Weather**. Did the weather shape the way life was lived in your community?

- **Industries**. Was there a predominant occupation in your town that influenced your life? Did most of the adults work at the same place?

- **Commerce**. What stores were available to you? Was there anything about them—the way they looked, the merchandise they offered, the way business was conducted—that would be interesting?

- **Population**. Was your community densely or sparsely populated? Was there a dominant ethnic, political, or religious group? Were people generally friendly and courteous? Were they prejudiced? How did people dress? What was considered acceptable behavior?

- **Transportation**. How did people get around town? What problems or benefits did this present?

- **Hangouts**. Where did young people congregate on weekends? What memories do you have of those places?

- **Entertainment**. What did people do for fun? Did they support home-town activities?

- **Religion**. Did a particular faith or sect influence the standards of behavior for your community? What were the effects? Did you fit in?

- **History**. How was your community settled? Did anything of historical significance occur there?

- **Crises**. Was your town a victim of natural disasters or economic ups and downs?

- **Traditions**. Did your community turn out for parades, sporting events, or county fairs?

- **Noteworthy achievements**. Was your area noted for any achievements— beautiful trees or gardens, championship basketball teams, a hometown girl who became famous? Did it boast of anything that was the biggest, best, or first in the region?

- **First impressions**. What would strangers notice the first time they came to your community? A scent in the air? A notable landmark? The weather? The noise? The quiet?

Capture What's Important to You

This is a fairly comprehensive list and not everything may apply to your locale. As you consider where you've lived, you'll undoubtedly think of other ideas. Try to be selective about what to include. If you try to incorporate too much information from this list, it will clutter your story and feel like an encyclopedia entry, which is not what you're aiming for. Instead, find a way to weave into your narrative those things that capture what was most memorable to you about your community and help your readers visualize it as you do.

Let's look at a few examples. The first is a description written by one of our students:

Diagonal, My Hometown

I grew up in a jerk-water town. Diagonal, Iowa, was so small you could drive from end to end in two minutes without rushing. The business district occupied two and a half blocks, flanking a macadam street. Someone once jokingly remarked that the town was so small the electric power company was a Diehard battery.

Diagonal had two claims to fame: the high school basketball team and the railroads. The basketball team won the state championship in 1938 and played in many state finals since then. Diagonal boasted two railroads. Their tracks crossed each other on the diagonal, which accounts for our town's name.

Many people apply the term "jerk-water" to any small town of little significance. Actually, the term has a technical origin connected with the railroads. In the days of steam, thirsty locomotives required frequent water refills, and nearly every small town had its track-side water tower. When the train pulled into a town, the locomotive fireman reached up to jerk down the water spout to fill the tank on the tender, hence the expression "jerk-water."

Jerk-water town or not, the entire community celebrated births, marriages, and achievements of all sizes. We also mourned together when someone died. A more friendly, honest and caring group of people could not be found anywhere. The visible face of the town has changed over the years, but the people and values have not. I am proud of my jerk-water hometown.[1]

In these four paragraphs, the author helps us see his Midwestern setting by describing the town's size, its close-knit population, its achievements, its mode of transportation. We also receive a brief lesson on the origin of the expression *jerk-water town,* which is helpful for the author's descendants who will read his account. The battery analogy is a good one, offering a touch of humor while making its point about the community's size.

An example from Lisa See's *On Gold Mountain* paints a convincing picture of post-World War II Los Angeles. She captures the optimism and prosperity of 1950s America.

"Look for resonance when you write about the places in your life. Your readers will bring memories of their own to your story and thereby, subconsciously, do some of your work."
—William Zinsser

> Not since the railroad pricing wars of the 1880s had Los Angeles experienced such prosperity and change. The first Christmas after the war, downtown was gaudy with lights and decorations and families together again. Department stores filled their windows with fantasy displays of everything from electric trains to washing machines. Santas, puffy with padding and fake beards, handed out strings of rock candy and lollipops to rosy-faced children. GIs still in uniform prowled the sidewalks in groups or honked their way down congested streets in their jeeps. Women, basking in the radiance of early pregnancy, window-shopped past the Broadway, Silverwoods, and Barker Brothers. At night, the women linked arms with men they'd thought they'd never see again, and stood in line to take in a movie at the Orpheum, Lowe's, State, Pantages, Paramount or the Million Dollar.[2]

The author has done her homework. Notice that she refers to specific stores and theaters that were popular at that time. Anyone who has been to Los Angeles will recognize that this city no longer exists. Think what future generations would miss if See had failed to create such a striking setting.

In his memoir, *Family,* author Ian Frazier shows us another way to describe a locale. The setting is Norwalk, Ohio, a town where one of his ancestors lived. First he provides us with geographical and historical details:

Norwalk, Ohio, is an inland town in an inland state. It is about 107 miles from the Pennsylvania border on the east and 112 miles from the Indiana border on the west. Its founders, for fear of fevers, did not want to live near swamps or river bottoms, so the site they chose was a long sand ridge above the forks of the Huron River, twelve miles in from Lake Erie. The town's population was about 7,000 in 1900, and it is 15,000 now.[3]

Frazier wants to fix his town in our minds geographically. He does so briefly. If he continued any longer in this vein, he'd lose our attention. Instead, he quickly moves on to other aspects of the community, providing a compelling description that helps us imagine the Norwalk of his story:

> Nights then were dark and quiet. If you were lying awake, you might hear the tread of a driverless horse hauling home his drunken owner, passed out in the wagon box. People rarely locked their doors, and when they did, they had to hunt all over for the key. Everyone knew everybody. Most would also talk without hesitation to any stranger who resembled themselves.[4]

Let your imagination help you re-create the atmosphere and feeling of your town, as Frazier does in this example. Try to remember what sights, sounds, and smells greeted you daily, then take your readers there—back in time. Consider, for example, what sounds you heard as a kid when you lay in bed at night. Thunderstorms? Cicadas? Lawn sprinklers? The ticking grandfather clock? What fragrances surrounded you on warm summer days? Honeysuckle? Newly cut grass? Cow manure? Pool chlorine? Good novelists know how to immerse us in the world of their stories with vivid "sense details" like these that enliven their setting descriptions. You can do the same with the places in your life.

Though it may seem obvious, we should point out that setting means more than just towns and communities. Everything we do takes place in a *setting*. As you describe incidents in your life, make sure your readers see the environment where it occurred. Perhaps you want to write about the time you and your older sister were washing dishes after supper and she suddenly confided to you that she was secretly engaged. As you describe the incident, give us a sense of that kitchen. It's not necessary to describe the entire room, of course, but select a few images—the galvanized tub that served as a sink, the warped wooden counter top—details that will help us visualize where that conversation took place.

One of our students wrote about an incident that occurred in his hometown in southern Alabama when he was a teenager. To set the stage for the story, he described his experience walking through a black neighborhood. Notice how his detail-rich account pulls us into that environment so we feel like we're walking beside him, feeling the heat, hearing the sounds, smelling the food inside the homes.

> We headed down the dirt street through the "quarters." Twilight had fallen, but the heat lingered. As we walked, sweat ran down my chest and soaked my shirt. Black families had finished supper and were sitting on their porches, trying to get relief from the oppressive heat and humidity of the Southern summer evening. They watched us two young white boys as we strolled through their world. Some waved and smiled. Some watched in curious silence, but said nothing. A few mumbled

softly to their barking dogs to be quiet. The smell of fried chicken and catfish still lingered in the night air.[5]

You remember descriptions like this long after you finish the story because of the memorable sense images.

Another student keeps a small sign at her computer monitor that reminds her to check her writing for images that evoke each of the five senses. Her stories are full of memorable sensory details as a result. Here's an example, a description of her impressions upon landing in her former home of Pittsburgh one winter morning after a flight from California, where she currently resides:

> We landed in a morning of dull purple shadows, in a place where noses turn red then white with cold. The airport smelled like hot dogs and stale popcorn. In the rotunda middle-aged men wearing high school lettermen jackets and brown corduroy pants stood in line to buy bratwurst and Iron City Beer for breakfast. Women in dark wool coats shuffled across terrazzo floors with their heads down and their knees bent, as if magnets in the soles of their boots anchored them to this place.
>
> I waited for the rental car outside of the baggage claim and watched a Clark Bar wrapper whip back and forth across the driveway. I sat on a cement bench and felt it drain my last memories of California sun. It's still Pittsburgh, I thought. It's like I never left.[6]

We'll end this section of the chapter with one of our favorite setting descriptions, one that always brings a smile to our lips because it's filled with the kind of humorous observations that are the stock and trade of true storytellers. It's

Garrison Keillor's description of childhood in his imaginary community of Lake Wobegon, a childhood much like ours, and probably much like yours.

> It was a good place to grow up in, Lake Wobegon. Kids migrated around town as free as birds and did their stuff, put on coronations and executions in the long, dim train shed and the deserted depot, fought the Indian wars, made ice forts and lobbed grenades at each other, dammed up the spring melt in the gutters, swam at the beach, raced bikes in the alley. You were free, but you knew how to behave. You didn't smart off to your elders, and if a lady you didn't know came by and told you to blow your nose, you blew it.[7]

We have provided you with a variety of examples that show ways you can re-create the places in your life. Practice writing descriptions that include what is meaningful to you about these locations. Enhance them with the kind of details that will help your readers see these places the way you remember them.

Where to Find Information

If you have trouble remembering details about places from your past, don't despair. There are all kinds of resources to help refresh your memory.

- **Newspapers**. Nearly every community has some kind of newspaper archive. Check the local library or newspaper office for bound or microfilmed volumes, or, in some cases, photographs or scans of the newspapers stored on electronic disks. The articles, opinion columns, and even advertisements from issues published at the time you lived there will jog your memory and provide a rich source of background information.

- **The Internet**. Most counties have websites that describe the history of the towns within their boundaries. Go to the *USGenWeb Project* (www.usgenweb.org) and click on your state, then your county of interest, or use a search engine like Google or Yahoo to find information about a locale.

- **Libraries, historical societies, chambers of commerce**. Many communities have some way of archiving historical information about their area. You never know what treasures you may find in these repositories, sometimes even information that relates to your family.

- **Family**. Take time to talk with parents, siblings, and other relatives about their memories of your hometown.

- **Old photographs**. Browse through old photo albums and look at the homes, the streets, the scenery in the background. Do you notice anything you could use in your descriptions of that location?

- **Field trips**. Visit the places where you lived and attended school. Drive down those old streets and soak in the atmosphere. You'll be surprised how many memories will spring into your consciousness with this kind of sensory input.

Learn by Doing

19. Draw a simple map of your hometown, identifying key sites that played a role in your upbringing, such as homes, schools, churches, local hangouts, and recreational sites. What special memories do you have? What do readers need to know to understand your circumstances there? After you've thought about these questions, write a description of this town that makes it real for your readers.

Learn by Doing

20. Try capturing the essence of your town in one colorful sentence. Garrison Keillor describes the fictional town of Lake Wobegon in the 1880s with this provocative sentence: "Lake Wobegon was a rough town then, where, all on one block, for less than five dollars, you could get a tattoo, a glass of gin, and a social disease, and have enough left over to get in a poker game, but Lutherans civilized it."[8]

Here's how one of our students completed this assignment: "I grew up in a Wisconsin town so small you could—with one vigorous sneeze—miss sight of the cows, banks, service stations, and U-Need-A-Lunch diner and find yourself on the town's outskirts, hungry and out of gas."[9]

21. Write a description that leads your reader on a "tour" of your community. If people were to drive into your town, what would they see first? What landmarks would catch their attention? What sights, sounds, and smells would they notice?

Notes

1. This was written as a class assignment by Es Ferris, of Palm Desert, California. It was included in his fine memoir, *Parallels to the Diagonal,* published in 2001 by Creative Continuum. Es passed away in March 2004.

2. Lisa See, *Gold Mountain*, 227-28.

3. Ian Frazier, *Family* (New York: Farrar, Straus, Giroux, 1994), 9.

4. Ibid., 9-10.

5. Excerpt from "Blue Moon Café," a story by Willie Walker of Orange, California.

6. Excerpt from "Going Home," a story by Bonnie Copeland.

7. Garrison Keillor, *Wobegon Boy* (New York: Viking, 1997), 2.

8. Ibid.

9. This was written as a class exercise by Thomas Murphy of Huntington Beach, California.

Chapter 7

Re-creating Your World

Establish Your Life Context

*T*hose of you who watch television's *The Tonight Show with Jay Leno* may be familiar with the host's "Jaywalking" segments, where he interviews people on the street and asks them to respond to questions about historical events. Their answers are often hilarious. Leno asked one college student, for example, "Who did we fight against in the Revolutionary War to win our independence?"

After scratching her head for a moment in puzzlement, the young lady's eyes lit up. "Russia," she answered, with a confident smile.

Other students couldn't say whether the Vietnam War or World War II came first. They didn't know whether the state of Washington was closer to Canada or Mexico. They were unable to correctly supply missing words in famous quotes, such as Neil Armstrong's, "One small step for man, one giant leap for _____."

Many of these same people demonstrated remarkable knowledge about topics such as popular culture. Most of us

chuckle and shake our heads at their muddle-headed responses to basic historical questions. We wonder how students can go through the American school system and have so little understanding about anything that occurred prior to 1980. While these interviews can be entertaining, they teach something important to people writing their personal histories. You must re-create the world in which you lived if you want future generations to understand what your life was all about.

For many young people, the world you grew up in will seem to be as foreign as the frontier prairie surroundings of Abraham Lincoln. When you ponder the speed and breadth of changes that have occurred during your lifetime, you can perhaps understand why today's youth may find it difficult to relate. Just think how transportation, communication, medicine, and social mores have evolved since your childhood.

For instance, you may have had an outhouse in your backyard or remember running outside to see an airplane overhead because it was such a novelty. You may recall when mustard plasters and castor oil "cured" almost everything, and when radio and newspapers, not television and the Internet, were a person's primary link to the outside world. You may have lived in a time before polio vaccine and bypass surgery. You may remember a time before cell phones and the Internet revolutionized communication and introduced a whole new vocabulary to our language. You may still think "river," for example, when you hear the word *Amazon* and "fruit" when you hear the word *blackberry,* while the cyber-savvy among us think "online bookstore" and "wireless messaging device."

Most of us grew up in a different world—a world that shaped our experiences, our choices, and the people we've become. You see how vitally important it is that you import these realities into your story. Otherwise, your readers may fail to comprehend an important part of why you are who you are.

Russell Baker makes this point in the opening chapter of his memoir, *Growing Up*:

> We all come from the past, and children ought to know what it was that went into their making, to know that life is a braided cord of humanity stretching up from time long gone, and that it cannot be defined by the span of a single journey from diaper to shroud.
>
> I thought that someday my own children would understand that. I thought that, when I am beyond explaining, they would want to know what the world was like when my mother was young and I was younger, and we two relics passed together through strange times. I thought I should try to tell them how it was to be young in a time before jet planes, superhighways, H-bombs, and the global village of television.[1]

For many young people, the world you grew up in will seem to be as foreign as the frontier prairie surroundings of Abraham Lincoln.

"All That I Am I Owe to ..."

Your life did not occur in a vacuum. Your personality, self-image, choices, happiness, and sorrows were influenced by a variety of factors, including some of the following:

Family Influences

- Genetics
- Birth order
- Religious views

- Socio-economic status
- Personalities and child-rearing practices of your parents
- Proximity and influence of your extended family
- Your parents' degree of contentedness in their marriage
- Educational level of your parents

Community Influences

- Community size
- Your family's standing in society
- Predominant ethnicity, religion, occupations
- Weather and geography
- Traditions and customs
- Prejudices

Regional and National Influences

- Natural disasters
- Politics
- Economic stability
- Inventions and technological advances

Life-Changing or Chance Events

- Catastrophes, natural disasters
- Economic fluctuations
- Illnesses, accidents
- Political traumas (wars, assassinations, scandals)

Personal Influences

- Character and personality traits
- Health

- Education

- Talents

- I.Q. and "street smarts"

As part of your writing preparation, you should consider how some of these factors may have influenced your life. You'll find it worth your time to review this list and reflect on the degree to which your environment contributed to who you are. Your personal history will feel flat and superficial if you report events without showing how they shaped your choices and identity.

Consider how much more interesting and comprehensible your life will be if you vividly describe, say, the rural community you grew up in—the one dominated by farming families whose lives were regulated by the weather, the price of grain, and the dictates of the local minister. Maybe you had a mother who didn't drive, who spent her days cleaning and cooking for her family, who entertained herself by listening to radio soap operas. Perhaps this family background made you yearn for more education, for life in a large cosmopolitan city. Perhaps it caused you to work hard in school to earn a college scholarship so you could get a desk job in Chicago. No matter what your life experiences, if you show what your world was like and how it shaped who you are, your readers will better understand what your life is all about.

Don't Take Anything for Granted

Your readers may not understand what you mean if you say that your mother was a housewife. What did it mean to be a housewife in "her day"? What did this entail? How did she perform her daily duties? What did she wear during the day? How did her life compare with other women in her community?

The same principle applies to other occupations. What did it mean to be involved in a certain line of work? What training was required? What kinds of tools were used? How long did it take to perform certain tasks? What were the benefits and drawbacks? What was the salary?

Likewise, elaborate when you describe your religious background. Don't just say you were "raised in the Lutheran faith" and expect your readers to understand what that means. What did Lutherans believe in your day? What were their traditions, taboos, and religious practices? How were people of your religion accepted in your school and town?

Be sure you define terms such as Black List, New Deal, Victory Garden, KKK, DAR, Gibson Girl, WAVE, New Wave, Flapper, Beatnik, Hippy, John Bircher, Dead-Head, Generation X, Hard Rock, and so on. Don't assume your readers will be familiar with these terms and acronyms.

Describe Your Home Life

Make your past come alive with details that paint a rich picture of what it was like to grow up in your house. Many

Learn by Doing

22. Describe what it was like to be a teenager in the town where you spent your adolescence. What did you do for fun? Where were the hangouts? What slang expressions were popular? What did you like and dislike about the town at that time? What made your town different from others? Capture the atmosphere with specific details.

of our students love writing about the various "vendors" who delivered goods to their homes. You may remember visits from the ice man to replenish ice in your Kelvinator. There were others like him—the coal man, the milk man, the Good Humor man—who played an important part in maintaining the rhythms of mid-twentieth century households. You likely have similar memories that remind you of how different your home life was from that of young people today. We find it amazing when we recall that insurance brokers and television repairmen actually made house calls when we were kids. Even doctors sometimes made a home visit in certain circumstances. My, how times have changed.

Kitchens and bathrooms also have changed dramatically over the last half-century. Maybe you had a coal-burning stove, incinerator, outhouse, or pull-chain toilet. Don't forget to include these vestiges of the past in your story.

What did your furniture look like? Did you have hardwood floors? Linoleum? Floor heaters? What was your bedroom like? Some of our students who were children during the Depression remember storing clothing in wooden apple crates rather than in chests of drawers. How many siblings shared your room? Your bed? Remember those old rotary-dial telephones and party lines? Can you recall any humorous incidents relating to them?

Former President Jimmy Carter grew up in Plains, Georgia, during the era of party lines. The following excerpt from his memoir, *An Hour Before Daylight,* entertains us with a peek at the nosiness of small-town life, while it anchors his childhood in a specific place and time:

> Very few farm houses had a telephone, but there was one in our house. It was number 23, and

we answered two rings. On the same party line, the Bacons had one ring and the Watsons picked up on three. (In fact, there were usually two other listeners to all our calls.) We seemed to have an omniscient operator in Plains. If we placed a call to Mr. Roy Brannen, Miss Gladys would say, "He left for Americus this morning at about nine-thirty, but he plans to be back before dinner. He'll probably stop by the stable, and I'll try to catch him there." She also had the latest news on any sickness in the community, plus a lot more information that indicated there were maybe three listeners on most calls.[2]

The rituals surrounding family meals change from generation to generation. What were meal times like in your home? Did you say a prayer of thanks before eating? What were your favorite foods? Were you required to eat everything on your plate? What did your family talk about during dinner? How was the table set?

Don't forget to include descriptions of how you entertained yourself before there were back-yard swimming pools, soccer leagues, computers, video games, and DVDs. Do you remember Kool Aid stands, the Good Humor man, jumping rope, or playing Hopscotch, Hide and Seek, Sardines, Kick the Can, or Hit the Bat? Can you recall the hours you spent playing with jacks, marbles, paper dolls, and hula hoops? Do you remember skating on those noisy, ball-bearing roller skates with a skate key swinging from a ribbon around your neck?

Many young people can't visualize any other kind of home life than the one they have. Help them understand your world by including a variety of interesting details from your childhood.

Don't Forget Pop Culture

What songs were popular during your dating years? Which ones were your favorites? Was there an "our song" in your life? What songs did you dance to? How did young people dance when you were in high school or college?

Similarly, you might consider the role movies, radio, magazines, and books played in your life. Dawn's mother remembers the impact the movie *Gone With the Wind* had in her community. She recalls that all the girls wore Scarlet O'Hara dresses to their school prom the year that movie was released.

What was it like to go to the movies when you were a kid? What was the price of admission? What did the theaters look like? What kind of treats did you buy at the snack bar? Some of you may remember the days when a uniformed usher directed you to your seat, her flashlight leading the way through the darkened theater. Were drive-in movies a part of your youth? Did you have any experiences there you could include in your story?

Were there favorite radio programs you couldn't miss? Did the family gather around the radio at certain times each week? Did you learn of any important world events, such as the bombing of Pearl Harbor or the fall of the Third Reich,

Learn by Doing

23. Write a story about the role of radio or television in your home life. What programs did you enjoy? What did the early radios (or televisions) look like? What stations were available? Are there any amusing anecdotes you can tell that will give your readers a sense of what your home was like at that time?

from the radio? Some of our students recall the terror they felt when they heard the broadcast of Orson Wells' *The War of the Worlds*.

What about the coming of television? Do you remember your first television set? What were your favorite programs?

While you're at it, don't forget clothing styles. When you describe the clothes you wore at different stages in your life, you create a sense of the uniqueness that reflects the time in which you lived. Homer Hickam does this well in his memoir, *October Sky*, in his description of the wardrobe preferred by popular high school boys in 1950s Coalwood, West Virginia.

When you describe the clothes you wore at different stages in your life, you create a sense of the uniqueness of the times in which you lived.

> I gulped down my hot chocolate and dashed up the steps past Jim coming down. Not surprisingly, Jim had every golden hair on his head in place, the peroxide curl in front just so, the result of an hour of careful primping in front of the medicine-chest mirror in the only bathroom in the house. He was wearing his green and white football letter jacket and also a new button-down pink and black shirt (collar turned up), pegged chino pants with a buckle in the back, polished penny loafers, and pink socks. Jim was the best-dressed boy in school.[3]

Notice Hickam's specificity here, the details about colors and the type of collar and pants, that gives his description the ring of truth. You probably remember how important these kinds of fashion statements were when you were young. Can any boy who grew up in the fifties forget the fashion necessity of "pegged pants" with that "cool" little buckle just below the back beltline?

What clothing fads were popular when you were in high school? What about those crazy hairstyles—marcels, bobs, flat tops, crew cuts, duck tails, beehives, French twirls, ponytails, mohawks, French braids, flips? If you were a teenage girl in the 1940s, did you wear leg makeup when stockings were unavailable? Did you wear white bucks, Mary Janes, t-straps, middy blouses, letterman sweaters, Bermuda shorts, hot pants, pleated skirts, poodle skirts, mini-skirts, sack dresses, capris, gaucho pants, hip-huggers, bell bottoms, or low-slung jeans? As you write about your school days, let your readers visualize your clothing and hairstyle.

As in any description, specific details are important, particularly when you're tying to capture the essence of certain fads. Be precise, mentioning brand names and titles, such as the Jade East cologne your girlfriend gave you for Christmas, the song "Misty" that played on the hi-fi when you fell in love, the Big Hunk candy bar you bought at the Red and White Market on the way home from school, the Helms Bakery truck that drove down your street each morning tooting the horn that sounded like a harmonica. Details like these ground your story in a specific era.

Notice in the example below how Garrison Keillor uses details effectively to resurrect the time and place of his youth in the fictional town of Lake Wobegon:

New Year's Eve passed without much notice, Mother and I trying for three years to stay awake by playing Parcheesi until one year we made it over the top to midnight. On the radio at eleven, Ben Grauer came on from Times Square to narrate the amazing descending ball of light that marked the

New York New Year, and Guy Lombardo and his Royal Canadians played from the Waldorf, which was exciting to imagine—the elegant Ben in a tuxedo standing on the rooftop watching the meteor fall, the handsome Guy and his band in their scarlet tunics like Sergeant Preston's, playing saxophones on horseback, their faithful huskies lying nearby—but it would have been more exciting to watch it on television, which we didn't have. At midnight our time, nothing happened. Mother and I hoisted a glass of grape Kool-Aid.[4]

Keillor succeeds in recreating an era by mentioning celebrities of the time, the name of the game he played, the beverage he drank. Do the same and you'll have an interesting story.

Include Current Events

Your life is remarkable for the historical and political events and developments you've experienced: presidential elections, wars, assassinations, political demonstrations, advances in medicine, transportation, space exploration, and technology. Not only should you mention these events in your story, you should explain how they affected you. Personalize them with anecdotes and feelings so they're vivid in the minds of readers who only know them as dry historical

Learn by Doing

24. Describe the way you dressed and wore your hair when you were in high school. Be specific so the era comes alive. Did you wear clothing that was "in fashion"? What influenced what you wore? How did you feel about the way you looked? The way others looked?

events. (See Chapter 8 for more about showing how your life intersected with history.)

But I Can't Remember!

Most young people are only vaguely aware of life beyond football games, pop music, and next weekend's date. It's only later you develop a broader perspective and become interested in what was occurring beyond your personal sphere when you were young. Suddenly you find yourself realizing your parents must have been worrying about money, all the while you were nagging them to buy you that pink angora sweater you saw in the store window. And how could you have missed that scary business with the Cubans in the sixties? While you were thinking you knew everything, you have come to realize you were missing most of it.

If you, like most of us, need a refresher course in what happened when you were growing up, you'll find books and web sites to educate you about the pop culture, social trends, and regional and national events that occurred during your lifetime. Here's a small sample:

Books

- McCutcheon, Mark. *Everyday Life from Prohibition through World War II.* Cincinnati, Ohio: Writers Digest Books, 1995.

- This Fabulous Century series. New York: Time-Life Books, organized by decade.

- Gordon, Lois and Alan. *American Chronicle: Six Decades of American Life.* New York: Atheneum, 1987.

- Lindop, Edmund. *An Album of the Fifties.* New York: Franklin Watts, 1978.

- Urdang, Laurence, ed., *The Timetables of American History*. New York: Simon & Schuster, 1996.

Newspapers

Newspapers are another valuable resource for contextual information for your life story. Check libraries where you lived and newspaper websites to determine the availability of archived issues from the time period you're covering.

The Internet

As you know, websites come and go, so we hesitate to recommend specific ones, but you can find them quickly enough with a search engine like Google or Yahoo. Just type in a topic, such as 1950s fashions, polio epidemic, or the Great Depression, and you'll access more information than you'll ever be able to use.

Learn by Doing

25. Choose an historical event that occurred during your lifetime and explain how it influenced your life. How involved were you with the event? How did you feel about it? Have your feelings changed? Did it affect the choices you made, then or later? Tell enough about it so future generations can grasp what happened, but be careful not to launch into an encyclopedic account that loses track of your story.

Notes

1. Baker, *Growing Up*, 16.

2. Jimmy Carter, *An Hour before Daylight* (New York: Simon and Schuster, 2001), 19.

3. Homer Hickam, *October Sky* (New York: Random House, 1998), 20-21.

4. Garrison Keillor, *Lake Wobegon Days* (New York: Viking, 1985), 236.

Chapter 8

Linking Your Life with History

Where Were You When ...

*W*hy were you born where you were? What prompted your family to move there? Why did you meet your spouse when and where you did? Why did you choose your career? Where did your ethics and values come from? Did "historical" events shape your answers to any of these questions?

Before you consider your answers to these questions, let's define what we mean by an historical event. In one sense, everything that has ever happened is historical. But in this case, we're referring to events that have general significance, the type that appear in history books, and can be researched in a library.

Some personal histories are written as though the author lived in a vacuum, offering no understanding about how his life fit within the context of greater history. What a missed opportunity and a loss for readers!

Future generations will find your story more compelling if they can link it with something they have read in history books or studied in school. They may even include your experiences in school reports or tell their friends about you: "My grandfather fought in World War II"; "My grandmother marched in Civil Rights demonstrations!"

Weaving this kind of material into your story may require you to bone up on some local, national, and social history to help your readers grasp what was going on in the world at the time.

Horrors! You may have been thinking that writing your own personal story would mean you could avoid study or research. But consider this: As we go about our daily routines, we're sometimes only vaguely aware of where we fit within the larger sweep of history. We're too close to developments and too preoccupied with other matters to understand how our lives are being shaped by the events around us. It's only when we begin to reflect from the distance of time that we can grasp how we fit into the larger picture.

If you can connect your personal experiences to a broader context, your story will make more sense and be significantly more interesting to your readers. The following example will illustrate:

Morris' father served in the Navy during World War II as a "SeaBee," a member of a construction battalion, or "CB." In the first draft of his personal history, he merely wrote that he had been stationed on the Pacific island of Tinian, and then he included a few personal experiences. What was missing was an explanation of how his presence in Tinian fit within the greater context of a strategy to defeat the Japanese in World War II.

In fact, it's quite likely that Morris' father did not fully understand these historical details at the time. The Navy

Future generations will find your story more compelling if they can link it with something they have read in history books or studied in school.

wasn't in the habit of telling every soldier and sailor the grand plan and how their individual mission might fit into it.

Since Morris had been asked to edit his father's memoir, he spent a day at the library doing research. Out of that came a number of passages that enhanced the original account. Here is the revised introduction to the chapter on Tinian Island:

> The Mariana Islands are located about 1,500 miles southeast of Japan. They became a key United States objective in 1944 because of their importance as potential staging sites for the conquest of Japan. Code named "Forager," the operation to invade the Marianas began June 14, 1944, one week after the landing at Normandy. More than 800 ships participated in the invasion.
>
> The main islands of the Marianas were Saipan, Guam, and Tinian. There was a month of heavy fighting before Saipan fell on July 9, 1944. Then attention was turned to Tinian. The Japanese organized fierce banzai charges, but by August 12, the last pockets of resistance had been eliminated and Tinian was secured. Nearly 5,000 Japanese soldiers lost their lives on Tinian.
>
> My SeaBees battalion came ashore on Tinian a month after it fell and we established our main camp in a sugar cane field. The officers' area was in a grove of papaya and banana trees. We soon began construction of seven airstrips capable of accommodating the B-29 bombers that were to be sent on missions to Japan. Each airstrip was nearly two miles long and as wide as a ten-lane freeway. Tinian was well suited for such construction. It was a rea-

sonably flat island, with no mountains, but there were fifty-foot bluffs around most of the ocean-front.

The United States would eventually send as many as a thousand bombers over Japan each day, and six hundred of those flew from Tinian. When we were finished, we had built the largest airport in the world![1]

The only portion of this introduction that appeared in the original draft was the fact that the main camp was constructed in a sugar cane field and the officers' camp was in a grove of papaya and banana trees. While this adds an interesting detail to the historical record, it does not give the reader any sense of the important role the island played in the war. With this expanded introduction, we have a more solid basis to evaluate and understand the personal recollections that follow.

"But My Life Doesn't Have Historical Significance!"

When we ask our students to evaluate their relationship

Learn by Doing

26. Many people divide their personal histories into "chapters" that begin with a major change in their life—a relocation, marriage, career advancement, career change, or religious conversion. Select a potential chapter in your life story and write an introduction incorporating the historical events that may have affected your changed circumstances. Think hard about this one—don't blithely dismiss the possibility that the change was sparked by outside influences. If necessary, spend time in the library or on the Internet learning more about the history of the time and place.

to outside influences, we frequently hear responses like, "I wasn't in the military. I haven't been politically active. My family's moves were motivated by personal factors, not historical ones."

When we hear excuses such as this, we can usually demonstrate otherwise by asking a few questions. For example, one of our students claimed that history had passed her by. "I was born in a little farming community in Idaho," she said. "Then my family moved to a farm in Oregon. I was vaguely aware of the Vietnam War, but none of my close friends were involved in it, and certainly nobody was demonstrating against it in our town. I just don't know any 'history' relevant to me that I could include in my story."

"Why did your family move to Oregon?" we asked.

The student thought for a moment. "Well, there was a whole area that had just been opened to farming, and my father thought it would be a good opportunity."

"What led to this area being opened for farming?"

Again the student thought. Then her eyes lit up. "Because the Grand Coulee Dam had recently been completed, and this brought irrigation to the area and made farming possible where it had been too dry before."

Bingo! Now our student had the beginnings of a wonderful bit of historical context. The Grand Coulee Dam was one of the marvels of engineering when it was built. A few hours in the library researching the factors that led to the construction of the dam, and the effects it had on agriculture in the area, produced enough material for a fascinating introductory section to set up the Oregon chapter of her life story.

"I'm Not Famous, So
Who Cares What I Think about History?"

Some of our students balk at the idea that they might have anything meaningful to say about big ideas or popular trends. However, if your readers are *your* descendants, they will want to know your thoughts and feelings precisely because you are *their* ancestor. A well-written memoir makes interesting reading for anyone. Historians love finding something written many years ago that presents a contemporary "ordinary citizen's" view of developments. History books are full of quotes from relatively unknown people who had the foresight to comment on issues of historical significance.

Morris had several ancestors who crossed the Great Plains with the Mormon pioneers between 1847 and 1860.

How was your life affected by these historical events? Where were you when they occurred? What was your reaction to them?

- The Great Depression

- The polio epidemic and Salk vaccine

- The first appearance of automobiles, airplanes, telephones, television, refrigerators, air conditioning, and computers

- The wars: World War II, Korea, Vietnam, Gulf, Iraq

- Assassinations of political leaders

- Deaths of celebrities or political leaders

- Political and economic changes

- Civil rights developments

- Changes in cultural mores

- The moon landing

Most of his ancestors apparently were too busy conquering the American West to leave any written remembrance of their experiences. Their histories, to the extent they exist, were written by their children or, more often, their grandchildren. As a result, the stories lack the immediacy and charm of a personal memoir.

One ancestor, however, a man named Edson Barney, wrote an autobiographical sketch later in his life, for which Morris is extremely grateful. Though only four pages in length, the sketch includes many interesting details that could provide the basis for a future, more complete, biography. In some respects, however, the sketch is like getting just one lick of an ice cream cone because it fails to provide concrete details about the significant historical events that Edson was part of or to offer any insightful commentary on them. For example, this is the sum of what Edson had to say about crossing the prairies from Iowa to Salt Lake City in 1850: "Nothing occurred on the way except a small Indian fight close by our wagons. Two Indians killed."[2]

Nothing occurred?

Edson walked the entire way as part of a wagon train trekking across the great American expanse at a time when hardship and danger were constantly present, deaths an everyday occurrence, every river crossing a perilous adventure, and buffalo herds still a threat, and "nothing occurred"?

Contrast Barney's cryptic summary with an excerpt from the autobiography of B. H. Roberts, another pioneer who crossed the same plains. Although Roberts was only ten years old at the time, his account, written years later, is full of wonderful anecdotes and homilies that make for delightful reading. In this example, Roberts explains what happened when he got tired of walking and stole a ride on the wagon:

[T]he freight wagon followed next to the wagon to which I and my sister were attached. The young man … who was the driver had a kindly disposition to help several of the young ladies in their march by linking his arm in theirs and guiding them over the rough walking beside the wagons. Early in the journey he had turned over the task of keeping the teams close up to the wagon ahead to me, so that I became at least part driver of the freight wagon team, which was drawn by four yoke of oxen.

On one occasion a night drive was necessary, and the young man was entrusted with the freight wagon team. The young teamster was unusually devoted to helping the young ladies, especially on this night, so I ran in behind the ox on the near side and climbed up on the seat that had been arranged in the front of the wagon by the regular teamsters. This seat consisted of a broad plank placed across the open head of a large barrel.

The day had been hot and the hours of the journey long, and I was decidedly tired, nearly unto exhaustion. Fearing that my riding, which was "agin" the law, would be discovered, I slipped the board from the barrel head and conceived the idea of dropping down in the barrel, secure from the eyes of those who might oust me from my seat in the wagon if I were found. To my surprise, if not amazement, I discovered when I let myself down in the barrel that my feet went into about three or four inches of a sticky liquid substance which turned out to be molasses. The smarting of my chapped feet almost made me scream with pain, but I stifled it.

Too tired to attempt to climb out, I remained and gradually slipped down and went to sleep doubled up in the bottom of the barrel, with such results as can well be imagined. It was daylight when I woke up, and there began to be the usual camp noises of teamsters shouting to each other to be prepared to receive incoming teams driven from the prairie by night herdsmen. As I crawled out of the uncomfortable position and with molasses dripping from my trousers, I was greeted by some of the teamsters and emigrants who caught sight of me with yells of laughter. I crept away as fast as I could to scrape off the syrup which added to the weight and thickness of shirt and trousers, for there was no change of clothing for me, and so bedaubed I had to pass on until dusk and drying somewhat obliterated the discomfort.[3]

Edson Barney certainly could have written stories like these if he had been instructed about the importance of providing details about his role in this epic migration—even if they were only humorous or seemingly trivial anecdotes.

All of us have lived through events that will be written about in future history books. Don't gloss over your connection with them. Make certain you give your descendants a compelling description of your opinions about local and world developments.

What Was Your Reaction?

Nearly all Americans who lived in the early 1940s can remember the day Pearl Harbor was bombed. Likewise, nearly all Americans who lived in the 1960s can remember where they were when President John F. Kennedy was shot or when the first man walked on the moon. The date of September 11, 2001, will be remembered by everyone who lived at the time and saw the destruction of the World Trade Center.

Most Americans born between 1940 and 1955 have strong feelings about the Vietnam War and the protests that it provoked. What was your view of the war when it was happening? Did you participate in demonstrations? Have your views changed since that time? Most people born before 1965 have an opinion about the Cold War, about communism, and about the fall of the Iron Curtain.

Most readers of this book have seen the introduction of personal computers and the rise of the Internet. Your descendants would find it interesting to know how you adapted to these new realities. In the beginning of the twentieth century, the automobile and airplane were equally new and strange, and it's difficult for young people to imagine such a world. As the digital revolution continues to change our lives, our descendants will probably look back and consider our current environment primitive or quaint and the people who lived through such times to be heroic. They will not be able to comprehend how people functioned without cell phones. Readers one hundred years from now will feel cheated if you fail to mention these developments in your life story and explain how you felt about them.

Have You Known Any Famous People?

You can enhance the appeal of your story by including encounters you've had with famous people, or people who later became famous. Read any good biography, whether of

"Your biggest stories will often have less to do with their subject than with their significance: not what you did in a certain situation, but how that situation affected you."
—William Zinsser

George Washington or Lee Iacocca, and you'll find refer-ences to people who knew these men and had experiences with them.

Almost everyone has rubbed shoulders with a famous person. By famous, we don't necessarily mean the president of a country or an Academy Award-winning actress. There are many sorts of famous people—leaders in education, reli-gion, the military, business, sports, entertainment, and liter-ature, to name a few.

If you knew someone before they became famous, so much the better. Your story can give a valuable insight into what that person was like in early life.

Morris' ancestor Edson Barney, mentioned earlier, knew Brigham Young and had untold opportunities to interact with him and other such pioneer leaders. He must have been considerably affected by Young and his message because, following the governor's instructions, he left his home sev-eral times to settle uncharted territory. How interesting it would have been had Edson devoted a few pages, instead of only a sentence or two, to describe his impressions of these influential men and his feelings about them.

Don't make your descendants wish you had written about the historical people you knew. Describe your experiences and share what you thought about them.

Don't make your descendants wish you had written about the historical people you knew. Describe your experiences and share your feelings about them.

Notes

1. Morris Alma Thurston, *Long Trail Winding* (Villa Park, Calif.: Thurston House Publishing, 1999), 162-64.

2. Edson Barney, unpublished manuscript, in author's possession, 3.

3. Gary James Bergera, ed, *The Autobiography of B. H. Roberts* (Salt Lake City: Signature Books, 1990), 31-32.

Chapter 9

The Hitchcock Factor

Rivet Readers with Conflict and Suspense

*A*lfred Hitchcock was a master of mystery. We have vivid memories from our youth of Saturday afternoons in dark theaters, palms sweating and hearts racing, agonizing over a plot development in Hitchcock's latest thriller. Hitchcock was a smash at the box office.

In the world of books, authors like Sue Grafton and John Grisham weave a similar magic, placing their heroes in jeopardy and their readers on the edge of their seats with novels that routinely top fiction bestseller lists.

People may fantasize about living carefree lives, but when it comes to entertainment, they want conflict and suspense. Why? Because exclusively happy stories are boring.

Imagine reading a novel about perfectly pleasant people who live one happy day after another, with absolutely no worries. How fun would that be?

Even children's books have conflict and suspense to keep youngsters entertained. Will Cinderella surmount the obstacles devised by her wicked step-family and make it to the ball? Will Hansel and Gretel escape from the witch and find their way home? Stories end at "happily ever after" for a reason.

When you sugarcoat, downplay, or omit thorny life experiences, you sacrifice honesty and lose reader interest.

Like novels, life stories also need conflict and suspense to hold the reader's interest. We all experience obstacles in life and, probably more than anything else, they shape who we are. Unfortunately, some writers gloss over unpleasant aspects of their past for various reasons. Some want to cast themselves in a positive light or spare others' feelings. Others simply fear revisiting unpleasantness by writing about it.

When you sugarcoat, downplay, or omit thorny life experiences, you sacrifice honesty and lose reader interest. When you dismiss your life struggles with cursory summaries—"Dad's temper kept his children at a distance"— you keep your readers at a distance, as well.

So, develop those conflicts. They need not be gut-wrenching experiences. Some conflicts could be as innocuous as competing in the sixth grade science fair. (Will you be the first girl to win the blue ribbon?) Or maybe you struggled with an adolescent crush in junior high. (Will she finally notice you after you get contact lenses and accidentally bump into her in the hallway?) Dramatize these human conflicts. Show how they affected your life, how you fretted and stewed, what you gained, what you lost, what the odds were for success.

Your life story should be filled with incidents that illuminate your hopes, dreams, worries, struggles, and traumas. Readers will love you for it, and they'll root for your success.

Give Your Story the Hitchcock Touch

What techniques did Alfred Hitchcock use to keep us spellbound? He made sure we identified with the heroes so we would worry about their safety and, by extension, our own. He created settings—dark, stormy nights, isolated hotels, and eerie quiet—that enhanced our worry. He took his time, letting us experience each new development through the eyes of his characters. He never telegraphed the outcome. He kept us watching and worrying to the very end.

That's how Hitchcock did it.

How will you do it? Do you think you could apply Hitchcock's techniques to develop the tension and conflict in your story? To give you some ideas, let's look at how other best-selling writers have done it.

Make Your Readers Worry

In Rick Bragg's memoir, *Ava's Man,* he writes about the time his grandfather was caught in a torrential downpour on a fishing trip. When Grandpa didn't return home for a few days, his family became sick with worry, imagining the worst. Instead of telling us this in a short summary paragraph, Bragg grabs our interest by creating an intense scene that puts Grandpa in the raging storm and makes us worry about him. Notice how he tells it from Grandpa's perspective.

> Later, as the sky started to darken, he noticed how high the river seemed to be running, so much higher than before....
>
> He also noticed that it was clouding up something terrible, and that the sky was changing from blue to a deep and angry purple, like it was bruised. Then the rain came at him like a waterfall.

"Drama is life with the dull parts cut out."
—Alfred Hitchcock

He ran to his car through the mud, and noticed that he couldn't tell anymore where the bank ended and the river began. He jumped in and tried the starter, and the thing whined and groaned but couldn't catch. Starters do that when you need them not to.

He tried it and tried it, the rain pounding and pounding at the roof, and the starter got weaker, fainter, and the water got higher, higher....[1]

When your readers know how situations affected you, you'll harness their sympathy and heighten the interest quotient of your story.

This is exciting stuff. It makes us want to read on and find out what happened because Bragg puts us close to the action. He paints a threatening picture that makes our anxiety grow. The river is running higher than usual. The sky is the color of a bruise, and the water slams into Grandpa like a waterfall, all expressions that create a feeling of uneasiness.

Bragg also uses repetition to build intensity. His grandfather *tried* and *tried* to start the car while the rain is *pounding* and *pounding,* and the water rises *higher* and *higher.* Repetition creates more tension than writing something like, "As the rain pounded with more ferocity, the water continued to rise."

Like Bragg, see if you can add details to your story so your readers can understand and visualize the gravity of the situation. Think about those ghost stories you heard around the campfire when you were young, the storyteller knowing how to add enough scary material to keep you terrified from moment to moment.

Show Your Goosebumps

Conflict provokes emotion. Be open about your fears, worries, anger, embarrassment, envy, competitiveness, or whatever feelings you experienced during hard times. When your readers know how situations affected you, you'll harness their sympathy and heighten the interest quotient.

Jennifer Lauck applies this principle in her memoir, *Blackbird: A Childhood Lost and Found.* Early in the story Lauck tells about the time her mother, on a whim, cut Jennifer's beautiful long hair into a short "European" style. Notice how Lauck creates conflict by first informing us that she loved her hair just as it was.

> My hair is dark brown, long past my shoulders, and it's mostly straight except for a little curl at the ends. You can do anything with long hair, ponytails, braids, barrettes. I love my hair.
>
> Momma picks up my hair, all of it in her hand, and I can see the shadow of her arm, the other hand with the scissors. My breath in, and one, two, three, my hair on the floor.
>
> My breath out, and I can't help tears in my eyes, my long hair like something dead on the green carpet. I touch the hair and it is cool and soft.
>
> B. J. comes up the hall and grins a big stupid grin, all the way into his dark eyes.
>
> "Wow," B. J. says, "you're practically bald."
>
> "Don't exaggerate," Momma says.
>
> "Well, short anyway," B. J. says.[2]

A few lines later, Lauck says, "It's not the end of the world, feels like it though, my stomach a wide-open hole with the end of the world falling through it."

Our hearts go out to this child because she shows us *her* heart. The author uses a variety of techniques to heighten the tension. There's a threatening shadow cast by the scissors and piles of cut hair that look like "something dead." Her brother adds to the strain with his snide comments about her appearance. Finally, she tells us her world is falling apart, slipping through the gaping hole in her stomach. Lauck shows us her goosebumps.

Another good example of how to make your feelings more palpable is found in Annie Dillard's *An American Childhood*, where she relates a family drama triggered by her letter to their preacher announcing she was quitting the church. Her parents are beside themselves with worry and embarrassment. Dillard communicates this state of mind by carefully describing how her parents reacted.

> What are we going to do with you?
>
> Mother raised the question. Her voice trembled and rose with emotion. She couldn't sit still; she kept getting up and roaming around the kitchen. Father stuck out his chin and rubbed it with his big hands. I covered my eyes. Mother squeezed lotion in her hands, over and over. We all smoked; the ashtray was full. Mother walked over to the sink, poured herself some ginger ale, ran both hands through her short blond hair to keep it back, and shook her head.[3]

This brief scene makes an impact on us because we can feel her parents' anxiety as they pace and fidget. Identifying such behavior heightens the drama and makes us feel their distress.

How did you react during various life crises? How did your emotions affect your behavior? If you merely say you were scared to death, you neatly summarize an emotional state but miss an opportunity to build tension and invite your readers into your life. If you show us your fear, embarrassment, or other emotions by describing gestures, posture, and actions, we are more likely to empathize with you.

Show What's at Stake

You add to the tension if you tell your readers what was at stake. What would have happened if you didn't win the scholarship? How badly did you need that job? What did winning or losing mean to you? What was the worst that could happen?

A documentary movie released in 2003 takes advantage of this principle. In *Spellbound,* we watch eight contestants' efforts to win the National Spelling Bee. Before the contest begins, we're introduced to each young person in carefully crafted vignettes that explain their difficult home situations, familial pressures to succeed, and the grueling and frantic contest preparations. In each case we come to understand what winning the spelling bee would mean for that person and their family. When the contest finally begins, we're on the edge of our seats. Only one can win, but by now we want all of them to win. We know these kids and understand what the stakes are. We're fraught with the same tensions as their hand-wringing parents sitting in the audience.

The same technique can be applied to memoir writing. Russell Baker shows us how in his memoir, *The Good Times.* Baker has completed college and needs a job. The following excerpt tells how much:

> On the phone I talked to a woman with a deep, snobby, go-to-hell voice, and she told me to come in for an interview a few days later. I took my only

"You don't know what it is to stay a whole day with your head in your hands trying to squeeze your unfortunate brain so as to find a word."
—Gustave Flaubert, letter to George Sand

suit to the cleaners for the high priced overnight clean-and-press job, asked my mother to iron my best shirt, and polished my shoes for the first time in weeks. It wasn't that I especially wanted to work for a newspaper. I was simply desperate for a job.[4]

Baker illustrates the tension by describing the aloofness of the receptionist and describing his obsessive preparations for the interview. By doing so, he enlists our sympathy and we follow the ensuing story with heightened interest.

Sustain the Suspense

One of the keys to Hitchcock's success was his ability to keep his audience guessing. He never gave away the ending.

You have the same potential to sustain suspense as you write about your own conflicts. Keep your readers wondering how it will all turn out. Will you get the promotion? Will you win back the love of your girlfriend? Don't show your hand at the outset with statements like, "If I'd known my sister could not be trusted, I would never have shared my secret with her." You will lose your advantage and ruin the excitement. Keep them guessing.

If there were roadblocks that hindered you from getting through a particular situation—adversaries, weather, health, time—play them up. Your readers will appreciate it.

Worry Them with Style

You can create even more excitement by using short sentences and paragraphs. This speeds up the pace and projects anxiety. Have your people speak in short, snappy phrases. Make them interrupt each other the way people do when they're upset and angry. Notice how Maya Angelou uses this technique in *I Know Why the Caged Bird Sings*:

"Usually, when people get to the end of a chapter, they close the book and go to sleep. I deliberately write my books so when the reader gets to the end of a chapter, he or she must turn one more page. When people tell me I've kept them up all night, I feel like I've succeeded!"
—Sidney Sheldon

"Miss Angelou, I am a counselor at Marvelland School and we don't think Guy should ride the school bus next semester."

"You don't thin … What 'we' and why not?"

"The principal, a few teachers, and I. We've discussed his action … and we agree—"

"What actions? What did he do?"

"Well, he used profanity on the school bus."

"I'll be right there."

"Oh, there's no need—"[5]

We've previously stressed the importance of choosing words carefully to convey a vivid visual picture. This is particularly crucial when trying to convey tension and conflict. Some words do it better. Choose strong, evocative verbs. "The storm clouds *boiled* on the horizon" creates more unease than "the storm clouds *grew* on the horizon." Similarly, writing "Mother *barked* at the salesman" heightens tension far more than simply having her *raise her voice* at the salesman.

Say you're writing about the time armed robbers broke into your home. How did you escape? Did you run out of the house or did you dash, race, sprint, charge, scramble, bolt, or dart? Each of these verbs invokes a different and more interesting mental picture than the more general *run*.

Verbs that enhance visual imagery will heighten the emotional impact of your story. Choose words that are more likely to stimulate your readers' imagination. Don't be satisfied with the first word that comes to mind. Obtain a good thesaurus and look for more interesting possibilities.

If you're having trouble identifying conflicts to include in your life story, consider the questions below. It's likely you have experienced several of the situations described.

1. Did you struggle to overcome a personal weakness or vice?

2. Have you wrestled with conflicting values?

3. Have you encountered difficulty reaching a long-term goal?

4. Did you ever experience a financial setback?

5. Did you have difficulties with relationships or matters of the heart?

6. Were there political or other external conflicts in your lifetime?

7. Have you been in dangerous situations?

8. Did you ever need emergency medical attention?

9. Did a loved one become sick or incapacitated?

10. Have you ever worried about survival?

11. Did you have to deal with extreme weather conditions?

12. Have you experienced tension in raising and guiding your children?

Notes

1. Rick Bragg, *Ava's Man* (New York: Knopf, 2001), 201.

2. Lauck, *Blackbird*, 101.

3. Annie Dillard, *An American Childhood* (New York: Harper-Collins, 1998), 235-36.

4. Russell Baker, *The Good Times* (New York: William Morrow & Co., 1989), 45.

5. Angelou, *Caged Bird Sings*, 141.

Learn by Doing

29. Write about a time when you needed something badly—money, a job, an honor or award, the recognition of another person. Carefully describe what you did. Reveal what was at stake and what emotions you experienced. Lead your reader through the entire episode, identifying roadblocks and looking for ways to build suspense. Choose strong verbs that intensify the tension. Don't telegraph the outcome.

30. Write about a time when you or someone you cared about was in danger. Recreate the incident as it happened, including specific details to heighten your readers' worry about the outcome.

Chapter 10

What's Essential and What's Not

Cutting the Clutter

*H*ave you ever known a person who tells stories that seem never to end? He tells you more than you want to know, venturing into needless details, going off on irrelevant tangents. He takes forever to get to the point—if he ever does.

You want him to finish. You shift from one foot to another. You begin to perspire. You "listen" and nod your head, but your mind furtively sifts around for an exit line.

Can life stories be similarly tedious?

Absolutely!

Like mind-numbing chatter, you can confuse and bore readers by including too many extraneous details that slow the pace of your story. For example, say you're writing about your family vacation to Hawaii. Do you give your readers a point-by-point description of the number of suitcases you packed, the time you left your house, the trip to the airport, the interminable wait in the ticket line, and the meals served on the plane? After all, those things were part of your trip.

125

Here's a quick answer: Unless something happened during the trip that's significant or exceptionally humorous or sets a tone for the whole vacation, fly your readers to Hawaii on the fastest, most direct route.

As you write about your life, memories will flood into your mind. It's exciting to recall people and incidents you haven't thought about in years. Should you include everything you remember so your readers will have a full sense of what your life is all about? After all, if you don't put it down, it may be lost to posterity. But would including everything make your story so tedious, few people would want to read past the first chapter?

What should you include and what should you leave out? This is a question that puzzles many writers.

Stick to the Guts of Your Story

If a story lacks punch and focus, it's probably because the writer is unclear about what he or she wants to say. This is forgivable—and really unavoidable—in a first draft because at this point you may not yet know what your story will be about. By the editing and rewriting stage, however, you need to become hard-nosed enough to axe any unnecessary digressions or tedious scenes.

Fuzzy thinking produces unfocused stories. Constantly ask yourself, "What does this incident add to the overall story? Does it tell something important about me or other people in my life? What is its point?"

For example, say you are writing about the time your grandfather refurbished an old bicycle as a surprise for your tenth birthday. What is the focus of this story? Are you try-

"Books aren't written— they're rewritten.... It is one of the hardest things to accept, especially after the seventh rewrite hasn't quite done it."
—Michael Crichton

ing to show the skill and creativity your grandfather used in refinishing the bike? If so, you want to describe what went into restoring it. But if your main point is to show that times were tough and the family had no money for new presents, a blow-by-blow account of how your grandfather fixed the bike would detract from your focus. If you're clear about the point of your anecdotes, the details are more likely to fall into place.

We help our students find what's essential in the myriad details of their lives by encouraging them to make lists before they ever begin writing. Try it yourself. Make a list of the stories that absolutely must be told—the ones you want people to remember about you. Make a list of the major turning points, often stressful times when your life changed direction and you had to make important decisions. These are just a few ideas. You may come up with others. This kind of methodical planning helps you zoom in on what's important so you can make decisions about what to include and what to discard.

Let's say you have noted details you recall about a favorite teacher. Some of the items on your list will be common to many teachers, but others will be unique to yours. You'll want to emphasize the unique points. Ask yourself what made her stand out from the crowd. What captures the essence of her looks and personality? What would strangers remember about her? When you're done, your description shouldn't sound like a missing person bulletin. Focus on what's essential to your story.

If you're describing your childhood home, readers don't need to know the precise dimensions of the rooms or the specific kinds of fabric used on the furniture. Instead, focus

"I notice that you use plain, simple language, short words and brief sentences. That is the way to write English— it is the modern way and the best way. Stick to it; don't let fluff and flowers and verbosity creep in. When you catch an adjective, kill it. No, I don't mean utterly, but kill most of them—then the rest will be valuable. They weaken when they are close together. They give strength when they are wide apart. An adjective habit, or a wordy, diffuse, flowery habit, once fastened upon a person, is as hard to get rid of as any other vice."
—Mark Twain

on the most memorable aspects of that house, the things that made that place a *home* for you. Shine a spotlight on these things and eliminate the rest.

Avoid Cluttered Descriptions

You may admire descriptions that are lush with detail, evoking images that engage all the senses. There's a point, though, when too many words become clutter. How do you know when you've gone overboard? Do you tell everything you know about a person, place, or event? Unfortunately, there's no easy answer. Often it requires developing an eye and ear for what works and what doesn't. This comes from practice and experience.

If you don't trust your eyes and ears, borrow someone else's. Our students often remark that they learn more about writing by reading their stories aloud in class. It's amazing what you'll "hear" for the first time just by reading to an audience. Often you'll realize you've overused certain words or phrases, even before anyone else calls it to your attention.

Inexperienced writers can become enamored with clever phrases and ornate sentences they've created. A pair of fresh, unbiased eyes can do wonders for flagging, unfocused prose that goes off track.

Read your story aloud to yourself. Your ears will hear what your eyes have missed. After you make your revisions, let your story "cool" for a couple of days, then read it aloud again. You'll be surprised what you notice.

Some writers think that good description requires lots of modifiers.

"I was working on the proof of one of my poems all the morning, and took out a comma. In the afternoon I put it back again."

—Oscar Wilde

It doesn't.

Don't overuse adjectives and adverbs. They add clutter and slow the story's pace. Consider this: "The unwashed, shaggy-haired homeless man walked haltingly toward the snobby, well-dressed woman." Look at all those adjectives and adverbs. Notice the pace-slowing commas. How about this instead: "The vagrant limped toward the socialite."

Usually you can find a noun that does the work of several adjectives. Ditto for verbs and adverbs. Instead of writing, "The dented old car went fast and recklessly through the place where the streets crossed," you could say, "The jalopy tore through the intersection." This conveys the same meaning but with more precision. Constantly analyze your writing to see if you have any pesky adjectives and adverbs

Learn by Doing

31. Review one of your stories for any non-essential clutter that can be eliminated. Does every sentence add to the story? Are there any paragraphs that can be shortened or deleted? Can stronger and more unique nouns and verbs eliminate some of those superfluous adjectives and adverbs? Be ruthless in your editing. Don't let your ego sabotage good writing.

32. Choose one of the stories you've already written and try shortening it by half. Has the story suffered by being shortened, or has it been improved?

33. Many stories lack the punch that grabs a reader because the author has taken too long getting it started. Examine introductions to each of your stories. Do any of them linger too long on unnecessary details or back-story? Notice where your story actually begins. If this point is far down on the page, move it closer to the top by rearranging or eliminating some of your paragraphs.

cluttering your prose that can be replaced with more descriptive nouns and verbs.

Streamlining Tips

There are two planning devices that help eliminate unnecessary digressions in your story: creating a chronology and developing a preliminary table of contents. While these may distract you from writing for awhile, they'll save time and frustration in the long run.

Assemble a life chronology

Creating a chronology, or time line, of your experiences will prepare you to write a more focused life story. To build a chronology, simply create a chart listing your most memorable events in chronological order. We suggest your chart contain three columns: one for the date, one for the event, and one for significant historical events that occurred during your life. Charts like the one illustrated on page 131 can easily be created in a word processing or spreadsheet program. Computers let you move entries around on the chart as new ideas come to you.

If you do not have a computer, three-by-five note cards are as useful. Write one life event on each card and include the date at the top. With cards, you can jot down ideas as they occur, then later sort them chronologically before entering them onto a chart.

What information should you include? The main events, of course: births, deaths, marriages, graduations, moves to new homes, achievements, illnesses, surgeries, vacations, accidents—whatever you feel was a milestone in your life. You should also include enough human interest items that your readers will get to know you—such things as your first kiss, the time you learned to drive, the fraternity prank you organized in college, that embarrassing experience with your in-laws.

What about the third column of your chronology? This is for historical events that occurred during your lifetime that may have influenced your life in some way. For example, Morris' father went to college and graduated in June 1941. He was married a few weeks later in July. Significantly, this was the same time Hitler's armies invaded Russia and just five months before Japan attacked Pearl Harbor.

Although Morris' father wasn't present at the Russian

Sample Life Chronology *(based on Morris' father's history)*		
Date	*Event*	*Historical event*
June 1, 1941	I graduate from Utah State University with a degree in civil engineering.	
June 30, 1941		Hitler's army invades Russia.
July 8, 1941	I marry Barbara Ashcroft in Logan, Utah.	
July 26, 1941	We move into an apartment at 34 Sudden Street in Watsonville, California. I begin working for the U.S. Soil Conservation Service.	
Dec. 7, 1941		Japan attacks Pearl Harbor
Dec. 3, 1942	I apply for a commission in the United States Navy.	

border or the naval base in Hawaii, these events would greatly affect his life, as they led ultimately to his enlisting in the Navy and spending several years in the Pacific.

Finding items to list in the third column will probably require some research. Few of us know our history well enough to tick off dates of events that occurred during our youth. Fortunately, there are many research aids. We have listed three in the box on the next page.

As we discussed in Chapter 8, including historical events in your story places your experiences within a larger context, adding interest and drama. To illustrate, here is a short excerpt from Morris' father's autobiography describing the period between his graduation and wedding.

> On June 30, 1941, Hitler's armies began the invasion of Russia—the most extensive ground attack in the history of the world—stretching over 2,000 miles from the Arctic to the Black Sea. As you might imagine, the war was making things rather unsettled for me as I graduated from college. I had registered with the draft board, but since America had not then entered the conflict, and since I was twenty-nine years old, I was not expecting to be called up soon.[1]

Adding historical detail like this accomplishes several things: It provides an ominous background to two otherwise happy events, it foreshadows his later decision to enlist in the Navy, and it connects his life to history in a way that will be fascinating to his descendants. Since his story was published, several of his grandchildren used the account of his World War II service for reports delivered in their school classes.

Constructing a three-column chronology may seem like a lot of work. It can be, but it is well worth the effort. In our case, we spent days building our life chronologies, creating charts that ran for pages. However, when we finished, we found we had created blueprints for our lives that guided the written portions of our own memoirs.

In some ways, making a chronology can be more fun than writing the stories. There is no better tool for triggering memories. As you assemble it, you'll begin to understand how you got from your childhood to where you are now. You'll see your life in the context of the world around you.

Your chronology will help you focus on significant incidents, turning points, recurring events, and general themes that are unique to your life. As you analyze it, highlight the items that most clearly illuminate what your life has been about. Consider including the chronology as an appendix at the end of your story to serve as a reference guide for readers.

"The beautiful part of writing is that you don't have to get it right the first time, unlike, say, a brain surgeon."
—Robert Cormier

Create a tentative table of contents

As you assemble your chronology, you will begin to develop ideas about how to organize your narrative. Try creating a tentative table of contents, keeping in mind that it's a work in progress that will probably change as you go along. You'll be surprised how sketching a rough outline will give you a sense of direction and commitment.

How should you organize your story? Most people present it chronologically, but that's only one of several possibilities. A common practice is to divide the narrative into chapters that focus on a major phase of your life. Here is a typical format:

• *Family background.* This chapter tells about your parents and grandparents and sets the stage for your birth. If you had older brothers and sisters, you might describe what went on in your family before you came along. If you know your genealogy back a few generations, consider briefly mentioning something of your ancestry, particularly if your ethnicity and heritage were significant influences in your life.

• *Childhood years (0-12).* In this chapter, you could tell the stories you remember from your childhood. If you have parents or older siblings still living, they can help you remember details. Did you have experiences that helped prepare you to become the person you are now?

• *Teenage years (13-19).* These are often difficult years, but rich in potential stories. Were you a troubled teen, or did you sail through these years without difficulty? Did you give your parents as many problems as your children have given you? What happened to you during these years that may have influenced your later life?

• *Young adult years (20-25)*. This is typically when enormous changes occur. Most people leave home and strike out on their own. This phase of a person's life may include college, military service, courtships, and marriage. In fact, so much happens that many people create separate chapters for each phase—a chapter for the college years, for example.

• *Settling down years (26-35)*. Now your wild oats have been sown and you may have begun to have children of your own, fixed on a career course, and come to the realization that you can trust people over thirty, even your own parents, who have suddenly become smarter.

• *Mature years (36-50)*. It is during this time that people tend to "make their mark" in the world. These are typically hard-working and productive years. Parents experience the challenges of raising teenagers. Some marriages fail. Other couples work through problems and solidify their marriages. Some move into a larger home or obtain significant advancements. Some become involved in community causes.

• *"Status" years (51-65)*. During these years many people reap the rewards of a life of hard work. Career people may have become managers. Your advice and endorsements may be sought for humanitarian endeavors. Parents see their children go off to college and create their own lives and families. Grandchildren arrive.

• *Golden years (66-??)*. These are the "retirement" years when people wind down and develop interests beyond their former careers. You may spend more time visiting children and grandchildren, attending weddings and funerals. People may also develop health problems. They begin to see their lives in retrospect and become more interested in writing their histories.

"Remember that you are a human being with a soul and the divine right of articulate speech, that your native language is the language of Shakespeare and Milton and the Bible; so don't sit there crooning like a bilious pigeon."

—George Bernard Shaw

These are merely ideas. The age divisions are arbitrary, based on a "typical life." As you construct your chronology, you may see other ways to divide your story. You may have lived in one place until age fourteen, for example, and then moved to an entirely different area. If so, the time of the move would be a better place to start a new chapter. If you have been married more than once, you will probably want to have a chapter division between marriages. If you have not been married or had children, your story will follow a different arc than someone who has. Let your chapter divisions correspond with your own unique circumstances.

You may find it easier to assign chronological divisions to your early life than to your adult years. Perhaps you pursued a particular interest or hobby during most of your adult life. Or you may have had a strong commitment to a church or community organization that spans several decades. In such cases, consider devoting a chapter specifically to those topics rather than weaving them into the chronological account of your life.

Some Final Thoughts…

It's generally easier to write long accounts than short ones. Creating a chronology and table of contents early in your project helps focus your thoughts and provide a structure for your story; however, don't let this process bog you down. Some people spend so much time on a detailed chronology, they never get around to writing the stories that are

Learn by Doing

34. Get more organized. Create a list of stories that must be told. Make a tentative table of contents. Begin compiling a life chronology.

at the heart of their lives. Your primary goal should be to get your story onto paper, no matter how wordy and unwieldy it flows out of your head. Then comes the pruning and polishing. Take your time with these tasks. It will mean the difference between a story that looks like it was penned by a novice and one that has the stamp of a professional.

Note

1. Thurston, *Long Trail Winding,* 141.

Chapter 11

Beginning with a Bang
Write a "WOW" Beginning

*I*f you saw the first Indiana Jones movie, *Raiders of the Lost Ark,* you've likely not forgotten how it began—with a series of heart-stopping incidents that threatened Indy's life at every hair-raising turn. He bested snakes, spiders, skeletons, and a monstrous rolling boulder before leaping off a towering precipice into the roiling waters below. It was a beginning to "wow" you, and one that left us panting for more.

It's hard to match a Stephen Spielberg opener. But we suggest you go for your own kind of thriller opening, one that announces, "Pay attention, this is going to be a great read."

The first pages of your story are the most important ones you'll write. How's that for intimidation? Like a handshake, your opener will say a lot about you and what is to follow. You've only got a page or two—sometimes less— to make a good impression.

Journalists refer to the opener as "the hook," which is

> *"One of the most difficult things is the first paragraph. I have spent many months on a first paragraph, and once I get it, the rest just comes out very easily."*
> —Gabriel Garcia Marquez

an apt term because your opener is what attracts the reader's attention. British novelist P.G. Wodehouse contemplates this issue in his humorous novel *Right Ho, Jeeves*. At the beginning, his main character, the feckless but lovable Bertie Wooster, ponders how to launch a story he is writing.

> I don't know if you have had the same experience, but the snag I always come up against when I'm telling a story is this dashed difficult problem of where to begin it. It's a thing you don't want to go wrong over, because one false step and you're sunk. I mean, if you fool about too long at the start, trying to establish atmosphere, as they call it, and all that sort of rot, you fail to grip and the customers walk out on you.[1]

To which we say, Right ho, Bertie! At some point, you have to come to grips with how to snag your readers. Your audience may excuse some sloppy writing later on in your story, but they may not even get that far if you haven't won them over in the first few pages.

Write to Get It Right

You may be wondering why we put a chapter about how to *begin* your story near the *end* of our book.

Here's why: In the course of teaching hundreds of students, we find almost all memoir writers need time to think and write about their lives before they discover the focus and shape of their story. Few begin the writing process knowing which stories they will end up telling, what themes will emerge, what form it will take. We generally save our "How to Begin" lesson until students have been writing for at least several months and sometimes several years. It's not until then that most people understand enough about their own lives to focus on the specific idea or anecdote that will launch their story.

Besides, with all that practice under their belts, they're bound to write a more compelling opening hook.

More Than Just Dazzle

Your opener does more than just grab your readers' attention. It establishes your style. It lets them know if your book is going to have a formal, academic feel, or one that is more relaxed and conversational. They learn whether it's going to be a gut-wrenching "tell all" kind of story, or one that will be more reserved in its approach.

Likewise, the opening pages typically establish the general theme, if there is one. Historian Doris Kearns Goodwin's memoir, *Wait till Next Year*, tells of her lifelong love affair with baseball. She establishes this idea in the first paragraph:

> When I was six, my father gave me a bright-red scorebook that opened my heart to the game of baseball. After dinner on long summer nights, he would sit beside me in our small, enclosed porch to hear my account of that day's Brooklyn Dodger game.[2]

As you read published life stories of various kinds, notice the opening pages. What do they tell you about the tone and style of the book? Do they arouse your interest and make you want to read more? Why?

For practice, let's consider what we learn from the first paragraph of Mary Cantwell's *Manhattan, When I Was Young*:

> "It was a queer, sultry summer, the summer they electrocuted the Rosenbergs...." That's how Sylvia Plath started *The Bell Jar* and how I want to start this. Because that's the way I remember my

first summer in New York, too. It was hot, and before we went to bed Allie and I would set our version of a burglar alarm along the threshold of the door that led to the garden so we could leave it open all night. Any intruder, we figured, would be deterred by that fearsome lineup of juice glasses, dented pots and pans from Woolworth's. Sometimes soaked in sweat and sucking in cottony air, I would wake and look toward the black rectangle that was the yawning doorway and wonder if we weren't being pretty stupid. But we would smother without that little breeze from the south, and besides, this was the Village! Afraid to take the subway, afraid of getting lost, afraid even to ask the women in the office where the ladies' room was (instead I used the one at Bonwit Teller), I felt peace whenever, after one of my long lazy strolls down Fifth Avenue, I saw Washington Square Arch beckoning in the distance.[3]

What does this passage tell us? Quite a lot, actually. Cantwell begins by quoting the opening line from Sylvia Plath's memoir, summoning an image of the execution of convicted spies Julius and Ethel Rosenberg. Why does she tie her description of the weather to a controversial incident? To grab us by the throat—to inform us that the story that follows will be neither bland nor syrupy sweet. We know this is an author who will unflinchingly speak her mind about herself and everything else.

Notice, also, Cantwell's use of detail—the juice glasses and dented pans that ward off intruders, the references to Bonwit Teller and Woolworth's—all of which ground us in place and time.

This is an opening that does what it's supposed to do.

Middles and Endings Make Better Beginnings

Later in the chapter, we'll look at various ways authors of biographies and memoirs begin their stories. Before we do this, however, we have some advice: Don't begin your story with your birth unless there were some extraordinary circumstance surrounding it. While plenty of memoirs and autobiographies begin this way, there is nothing that makes readers' eyes glaze over more quickly than life stories that begin with "I was born in Batavia, Iowa, on March 4, 1928." Readers want something that excites them at the start, so get yourself born in chapter two.

It's usually far more engaging to begin your story somewhere in the middle or toward the end of your life. Consider opening with one of your life's high points or at a turning point that changed your life. Margaret Thatcher began *The Downing Street Years* at the moment she learned she had been elected Britain's first female prime minister. Morris began his biography of his ancestor Tora Thurston with a scene dramatizing Tora's decision to emigrate from Norway to the United States, a decision that altered his life forever.

Is there a particular moment or incident that captures the meaning and importance of your life? Dawn asked this question in one of her classes. A student who had a career with NASA said he would have trouble choosing one incident. After some discussion, Dawn said, "Was there a specific time you realized you wanted to be involved in the aerospace industry?"

The student thought a moment, then his eyes lit up with recognition. "Yes," he said, "when I got my pilot's license."

"Then why not begin at that point," she suggested.

It's usually far more engaging to begin your story somewhere in the middle or toward the end of your life. Consider opening with one of your life's high points or at a turning point that changed your life forever.

Toy with Different Approaches

The verb *toy* means to be playful, to experiment, to have fun. After you've chosen the moment or incident that will open your life story, play around with different writing approaches. Don't be satisfied with the first idea that pops into your head. Some writers, particularly beginners, are afraid to experiment. They feel relieved to get something down on paper, and they worry they won't be able to come up with anything else. Not true. Relax and have fun with your writing. Try an informal, chatty tone. Try saying something startling and audaciously honest. You'll be surprised how freeing this will be to your creativity and your writing in general.

Consider a straightforward, expository style, then change it, turning the same information into a scene. Scenes work particularly well as beginnings because they plunk readers right down into the middle of your life.

Below are two drafts from one of our students. In the first, she writes in an expository style, describing events that led up to her birth. The second example transforms the same information into a scene. Which do you find more interesting?

My Canadian Roots (1st Version)
by Marjorie Carter

I wasn't supposed to be born in Canada, but I was. My parents, Beatrice McMurray Wyluda and Edward Joseph Wyluda, lived in Bayonne, New Jersey, with my father's parents. Stephanie Santorwski Wyluda and Joseph Wyluda. The neighborhood they lived in was comprised mainly of Polish immigrants cluttered around a Polish Catholic church,

Mount St. Carmel's. Here the congregation could worship and learn in their native language. The church and school were just over the back fence from my grandfather's home. The plan was that I would be born in the nearby Catholic hospital. But fate intervened.

My maternal grandmother, Hannah Cobley McMurray, was going to have surgery for a kidney removal in London, Ontario, Canada. In 1929 this was a serious surgery and required a lot of post-operative care. The Depression was a couple of months old now, and my grandfather didn't have enough money to hire a nurse. My mother decided to return home and help out. Since she was in her seventh month of pregnancy, this was not an easy task. Nevertheless, she boarded a train and headed for London. The bumpy ride must have been uncomfortable, but at nineteen she could handle it. She arrived early in December, ready to take on the task.

This is a competent opening. It creates interest because it sets a pregnant woman, the author's mother, in a perilous situation. However, the writing style feels stilted and overly careful; with so much attention to names, dates, and places, the story suffers as a result. All the genealogical information keeps us from becoming involved in the lives of the people. Notice how these problems are corrected in the author's second version.

My Canadian Roots (2nd Version)
by Marjorie Carter

"Bea, are you sure you need to leave right now?" asked Eddie. "I'm worried about you."

Eddie stood there with his arm around his very

pregnant wife, one shabby suitcase at their feet. The sounds of the trains approaching and leaving muffled his words. The two teenagers looked small and too young in the middle of Grand Central Station. He had tried to convince Bea not to leave from the time they left their home in Bayonne, New Jersey. Bea felt she must get to London, Ontario, Canada.

"Oh, Eddie, I'll be okay. Mama needs me. Her kidney operation is in a couple of days and I need to take care of her while Dad's at work. Don't worry about me. I'll be home for Christmas."

Eddie looked tenderly at his wife. "But, honey, our baby will be here next month. I don't want anything to happen to you or the baby. I need to be with you," he said.

"Nonsense, everything will be fine," Bea said. "I promise you."

Her train approached. They clung to each other as close as her pregnancy would allow.

"All aboard," the conductor called. Bea clumsily boarded the train, found her seat and waved goodbye, her face flattened against the window. Then the tracks carried her out of the station and on the way to London.

Her promise would be broken.

Rather than just names on the page, Bea and Eddie have become real people in the second draft. They worry. They love each other. We feel their youth and inexperience. We learn a little about their personalities by what they say to each other. The scene makes this possible. The author can provide us with their full names and relevant dates in an expository section later—or she can include them in a pedi-gree chart in the appendix if she chooses.

Don't overwhelm your story with names and dates and places. Those who do may create a helpful resource for family genealogists, but they won't have a page-turner.

Which Beginning Grabs Your Attention?

We have discussed two ways to open your memoirs with an engaging hook: beginning with a high point in your life and beginning with a scene. Now let's look at some other options. Perhaps you'll find an approach that will seem appropriate for the particular tone and structure you want to adopt. Any of them can be used to begin your story with a bang.

The Stephen King approach

Mystery writer Stephen King and others of his genre hook readers at the outset with suspense: an accident happens on a desolate, snowy road; a mysterious stranger arrives in town; a letter arrives out of the blue. Most of us love these kinds of openers, and we read on to see how it all turns out. Life stories can follow suit, focusing on an anecdote, a family secret, a crisis of some kind that piques the reader's curiosity.

Maxine Hong Kingston engages our attention in this way in her memoir, *Woman Warrior: Memoirs of a Girlhood among Ghosts*, which opens with:

> "You must not tell anyone," my mother said, "what I am about to tell you. In China your father had a sister who killed herself. She jumped into the family well. We say that your father has all brothers because it is as if she had never been born."[4]

Kingston's opening grabs our attention. We are drawn into the story because we want to learn more about this secret family tragedy.

The James Michener approach

Michener opens his novels with detailed historical and geographical discussions about his novel's setting. For instance, *Hawaii* opens with the sentence, "Millions upon millions of years ago, when the continents were already formed and the principle features of the earth had been decided, there existed, then as now, one aspect of the earth that dwarfed all others."[5] He then goes on to discuss the Pacific Ocean, the development of volcanoes, the settlement of the Hawaiian Islands—all this before he begins his story. Readers who enjoy this approach find the background information establishes context for the story that follows.

Some people are put off by all this "atmosphere stuff," as Bertie Wooster called it. They skip over it and start reading where the action begins. Be careful when choosing this approach that you don't overwhelm your readers with too much setting at the outset. Michener knew how to make it work. If you select this option, make sure it successfully launches your story.

There are a number of well-written memoirs and autobiographies that begin by describing the setting. Jimmy Carter opens *An Hour Before Daylight* with a word-picture of the terrain and landmarks one would encounter on a drive from Savannah to Plains, Georgia. Carter writes about this region beautifully, and by the third page he begins to narrow his focus to the particulars of his own farm, thereby drawing us into his boyhood life.

Jill Ker Conway begins *The Road from Coorain* with a chapter describing the western plains of New South Wales. The long description works because it's important that readers understand both the appearance and the emotional and physical demands of this environment if they are to appreciate the magnitude of what happens to the author's family. Conway is an expert at evoking the sights, smells, and sounds of the Australian landscape, and her opening chapter is a pleasure to read.

The Geraldo Rivera approach

Some say we've become a society of exhibitionists and "Peeping Toms." In recent years, memoirs have become increasingly frank about the private lives of their authors. Maybe it's our media mentality with its "reality" programs, daytime "shock" shows, and "infotainment" news hours. Whatever the reason, many of today's memoirs are noteworthy for their candid revelations about skeletons once securely locked in family closets. While some are written to appeal to a voyeuristic urge, many have literary merit. They generally announce by their tone and content in the first few pages that they belong to this genre.

Take Mary Karr's *The Liar's Club: A Memoir,* for example. This is a gritty story about growing up in a family of drunks, liars and psychotics. Karr's opening paragraph establishes the tone.

> My sharpest memory is of a single instant surrounded by dark. I was seven, and our family doctor knelt before me where I sat on a mattress on the bare floor. He wore a yellow golf shirt unbuttoned so that sprouts of hair showed in a V shape on his

chest. I had never seen him in anything but a white starched shirt and a gray tie. The change unnerved me…. "Show me the marks," he said. "Come on now, I won't hurt you."[6]

The Hamlet approach

Some memoir writers interject themselves into their beginnings, ruminating with their readers about the process of writing their story, discussing their struggles and purpose for writing. This approach establishes intimacy, the author addressing the reader as a trusted confidante. Helen Keller begins her autobiography, *The Story of My Life,* in this vein:

> It is with a kind of fear that I begin to write the history of my life. I have, as it were, a superstitious hesitation in lifting the veil that clings about my childhood like a golden mist. The task of writing an autobiography is a difficult one. When I try to classify my earliest impressions, I find that fact and fancy look alike across the years that link the past with the present. The woman paints the child's experiences in her own fantasy. A few impressions stand out vividly from the first years of my life; but "the shadows of the prison-house are on the rest." Besides, many of the joys and sorrows of childhood have lost their poignancy; and many incidents of vital importance in my early education have been forgotten in the excitement of great discoveries. In order, therefore, not to be tedious I shall try to present in a series of sketches only the episodes that seem to me to be the most interesting and important.
>
> I was born on June 27, 1880, in Tuscumbia, a little town of northern Alabama.[7]

It can be interesting to learn why people choose to write

their personal histories and what choices and challenges they encountered in the writing process. Most choose to include this kind of information in a separate introduction, while a few, like Keller, are effective in making it their hook.

The Benjamin Franklin approach

Has a specific principle guided your choices throughout your life? If so, perhaps you will want to begin by stating that principle up front. Here's a hypothetical modern twist on a Benjamin Franklin theme:

> My parents drummed the work ethic into us kids from the time we could walk. "Get out and make something of yourself" rang in my ears throughout my childhood. I hated it then. But now, looking back, I see that their teachings helped me become the billionaire I am today.

You get the idea. From there the author can continue his story with anecdotes showing how this principle influenced his life.

So, How Will You Begin?

You might start at the beginning with your birth. (We hope not.) You could grab your readers with a humorous anecdote that promises more entertainment to follow. You might relate a life-changing event that formed your thinking and choices thereafter. You could open with a statement of philosophy that guided the way you led your life. The list of questions in the box on page 153 is designed to help you determine which opening will work best for you. Consider your answers and see if they don't point you toward your own "WOW" beginning.

Notes

1. P. G. Wodehouse, *Right Ho, Jeeves* (New York: Penguin Books, 2000), 1.

2. Doris Kearns Goodwin, *Wait till Next Year* (New York: Simon and Schuster, 1997), 13.

3. Mary Cantwell, *Manhattan, When I Was Young* (New York: Penguin Books, 1995), 9.

4. Maxine Hong Kingston, *Woman Warrior: Memoirs of a Girlhood among Ghosts* (New York: Alfred Knopf, 1976), 1.

5. James A. Michener, *Hawaii* (New York: Fawcett Books, 1994), 1.

6. Mary Karr, *The Liar's Club: A Memoir* (New York: Penguin Books, 1995), 3.

7. Helen Keller, *The Story of My Life* (New York: Bantam Doubleday Dell, 1991), 1.

Learn by Doing

35. If you have completed most of the exercises in this book, you are ready to try writing a beginning for your life story. Review the questions on page 153. Make a list of possible ways to begin. Experiment with different approaches. Read two or three of your favorites out loud and see which one grabs you.

36. Select an incident or event that represents a high point or turning point for you and tell the story from beginning to end. Read what you've written, find the story's climactic moment, and consider beginning your story at that point. Will it grab your readers' attention?

37. Write your beginning as a scene, as Marjorie Carter does earlier in this chapter. Put words in the mouths of your characters and let them talk to each other. Bring them to life by giving them something to do when they talk. Let your readers "see" the setting where the scene occurs.

Questions to Ponder

- Have there been any recurring events or situations in your life that might serve as a theme for your story (travels, achievements, romances, hobbies, disappointments, handicaps)?

- Has there been a principle or philosophy that guided your choices?

- What was your greatest conflict?

- If people were to summarize you in a sentence, what would they say?

- Is there an incident that captures what you want to articulate about your life?

- Do you want your story to be "life affirming" in tone, showing your descendants you were positive and courageous? Is there an incident that establishes this theme?

- Is your story a tell-all, get-it-off-your-chest kind of piece? What incident would establish this tone right up front?

- What was your most significant turning point?

- What do you want readers to know about you on the very first page?

- Does your life include some kind of mystery or suspenseful incident that could be used as an introduction?

- What kind of story beginnings do you enjoy most?

Chapter 12

Jump-Starting Your Imagination

Story Ideas for the Stumped

*E*ach chapter of this book has introduced a technique to help you write a story as interesting as the life you've led. You've learned ways to write about people and places so your readers can visualize them. You've learned the importance of placing your life in the historical and cultural context of your times. You've seen how suspense, conflict, and snappy beginnings can grab and hold the reader's attention, how scenes and dialogue can show what it was like to be in your shoes at a particular place and time.

Now that you have these tools in your arsenal, all you need to do is write! We hope you've been writing as you've been reading, trying out these techniques by completing the Learn by Doing exercises in each chapter. (You'll find a complete listing of these exercises in the appendix.) They are designed to help you practice one writing technique at a time as you generate small portions of your life story. Even if you were a diligent student and completed all of the exercises in this book, there will still be large sections of your life you have not covered. Where do you go from here?

If you're like some of our students, you may still be at a loss for what to write about. Perhaps you can't remember certain portions of your life or you have trouble seeing the stories in your experiences. When our students report such problems, we give them writing prompts, a topic or a series of questions to write about. These little assignments nearly always help jump-start sluggish mental engines.

So in this chapter, you'll find a grab-bag of writing prompts to draw from when you can't think of what to do next. We offer them with this caution: It will be tempting to answer these questions in a general, summary fashion. Don't succumb to that pitfall! Focus on specific incidents. Tell *stories* that illustrate what you're trying to get across. Create *scenes* to illuminate important people in your life. Experiment with all the techniques you've learned to this point. In other words, *breathe life* into your story.

Bearing this in mind, see what you can do with the following topics.

Your ancestors

What do you know about your forebears? Have you or a relative researched your family genealogy? Don't devote a lot of space to giving names and dates. You can cover that in an appendix. Instead, consider how your ancestors may have influenced your life. Were any of them politicians, shopkeepers, teachers, miners, farmers? Did you follow in their footsteps? Do you feel their occupations or religion impacted you? Did you deliberately try to steer a different course? Did your ancestors follow the traditional paths of immigration? For instance, did your ancestors come from

Germany and settle in Pennsylvania, from Norway and settle in Minnesota, from Puerto Rico and settle in New York? Do some research and try to place them in a broader historical context. Look for stories to tell. Are there inspirational stories about your ancestors overcoming obstacles? Are there skeletons in your ancestral closet? If so, bring them out and tell us what they mean to you.

"If you can't get rid of a family skeleton, you might as well make it dance."
—George Bernard Shaw

Your parents

Parents generally have more influence on our lives than anyone else. Who were your parents and what made them unique? Has your opinion of them changed over time? What did they teach you? What did you learn from them? Which of their personality traits did they pass on to you? Which traits did you try to avoid acquiring? Don't just summarize their personalities—tell stories that illustrate who they were.

Your birth

None of us is qualified to write about his own birth, of

Learn by Doing

38. If you have completed Exercise 6, you already have a list of five to ten life-altering events that must be part of your history. As you read through this chapter, whenever you think of a story that might be included in your history, describe the event in a summary sentence or two. When you are finished with the chapter, you should have a considerably longer list of potential stories. Look it over and assign a ranking to each one based on how interesting you feel the story will be to your readers, perhaps designating those with the most potential with the number "1" and those with the least potential with a "3." Write those pieces with the most potential first. From this core list, you can probably progress through much of your life story. Refer back to the list as you continue to write.

Don't just mention somebody because you feel they shouldn't be left out. Have a reason for including a character in your story.

course. If your parents are still living, interview them to get details from which to construct a story. If your parents have passed away, are there any living people—aunts, uncles, or older siblings—who may remember details about your birth? Don't forget historical context. Why were you born where you were born? You'll probably need to do some research here.

The houses where you lived

If you lived in a particular house for much of your childhood, it's likely a treasure trove of memories for you. This house will serve as a setting for many of the stories you tell. Paint a word picture of the house so your readers will understand the physical environment. Pay particular attention to details that set the house within its time and place. What was the kitchen like? What sort of appliances were there? What chores were you given as a child? Did you ever try to sneak in or out of a window to avoid detection by your parents?

The places where you grew up

Give your readers a picture of your hometown. What was it like when you lived there? Go to the library and do some research to help bring back memories. Draw a map of your neighborhood, showing where other family members or close friends lived, where you went to school, where you played, where you went shopping. Don't be afraid to use the names of streets, parks, schools, and the like. Using place names will give your narrative the mark of authenticity. See Appendix C for an illustration of a neighborhood map.

Memorable relatives and friends

What people, aside from your parents, have most influenced your life? Was it a sibling, an aunt or uncle, a long-time friend? Let your readers see the uniqueness of these important people. Don't introduce them all at the same time. Scatter them throughout your story. And don't mention someone because you feel he shouldn't be left out. Have a reason for including a character in your story. Explain how he influenced your life. Better yet, tell us a story to *show* us his influence. Why is this person memorable to you? Have your feelings about this individual changed during the course of your life? Were there conflicts between you and this person? Were those conflicts resolved? How?

Principal antagonists

Have there been any people against whom you had to struggle? Did you have a demanding father? An overprotective mother? A boss who demeaned you? A sibling or friend with whom you constantly quarreled? Tell about them and your relationship with them, but avoid self-pity and, above all, be fair! Generally when two people have a conflict, there are two sides to the story. If someone has treated you poorly, there's usually a reason. Try to determine what it was and make sure you explain it in your story. This will make you more credible (and more likeable) to your readers. Did you grow as a result of your conflict? Was your life altered? How?

High school

Of course, everyone will want to reminisce about high school experiences. This was undoubtedly a critical time in your life. What classes appealed to you? Which ones did you hate? Did high school preferences play a role in determining what profession you later pursued? What clubs or cliques did you belong to? Were you with the "in" group, or an outsider? What sports did you play? Were you a good student? Did you receive any awards or recognitions? How did you earn money while you were in school? How was your romantic life? Did you learn anything from it? Did you have a steady boyfriend or girlfriend? Did you find it difficult to maintain the standards you had been taught at home? What kind of clothes did you wear?

"Don't overlook those seemingly small stories in your life that shaped the person you turned out to be."
—William Zinsser

College

Do you have an advanced degree? If so, give similar types of information about your college or postgraduate years. How did you finance your education? Where did you live while you attended college? Did you know at the start what you wanted to focus on or did you come to understand this during the course of your studies? Who were your favorite and least favorite professors? If you lived away from home, did you get homesick? Were you more intent on getting good grades or having a good time? What would you do differently if you were to begin school again?

Summer jobs

When you were a teenager, did you have a job during the summer? How did that job affect your growth? Did you learn the value of hard work? Did it give you a start on what was to become your career? Did it convince you that you wanted to avoid doing that sort of work when you grew up?

When Morris was a teenager, he spent a couple of summers working on a survey crew in the San Fernando Valley in Southern California. Temperatures were often above 100 degrees. The work was performed on dry asphalt streets or dusty, brambly hillsides. Based primarily on this work experience, Morris vowed he would get enough education to be able to work in an air-conditioned office. Other people find their temporary employment to their liking and set their sights on that field of work as a future goal. What did you take away from your part-time or summer employment experiences?

Turning points

We have all had turning points in our lives—junctures where our life's course may have taken a different route. It could be when we decided to go to college, marry, change jobs. Take some time to make a list of these life-altering choices. They will provide the basis for some of the most important stories in your book. Often they will suggest chapter divisions. For instance, if you had been drifting from job to job as a young person and finally decided to go back to school to get an education, you may want to start a new chapter to cover your school experience.

Major illnesses or accidents

Most people have suffered minor medical setbacks or have been involved in an accident. In your case, has anything occurred that materially affected your life? Tell how it came about and how you felt during your recuperation, what challenges you faced in order to get on with your life. Did you decide to pursue a different course than you might otherwise have? What did you learn from this? For instance, the great cyclist Lance Armstrong attributed his success in part to the cancer that nearly destroyed him. He realized that life is short and re-dedicated himself to his sport. As almost everyone knows, he went on to win an unprecedented seven

"By writing much, one learns to write well."
—Robert Southey

titles in the Tour de France. How did your life change as a result of factors over which you initially had no control?

Near-death experiences

Some people have come close to death through a narrowly avoided tragedy. If you have had such an experience, turn it into a story. Take your time and provide some background to build suspense. How did you feel when you realized you were still alive?

Humorous incidents

For some, humor is extremely difficult to write; for others, it comes naturally. But even if you find it difficult, try to include some wry observations in your stories. You'll find that some situations that seemed pretty bleak at the time now strike you as absurd or ironic in retrospect. That was the genius of Frank McCourt's *Angela's Ashes,* a Pulitzer Prize-winning memoir about a miserable childhood in Limerick, Ireland. Remember that the best humor is self-deprecating, so don't be afraid to laugh at yourself. If you don't see yourself as a comedian, don't try for big belly laughs. Stick to understatement, which sometimes makes for the best comedy anyway.

"Tension is wonderful for making people laugh."
—John Cleese

Stressful experiences

Have you sometimes had to do things you found extremely stressful? What and why? Supply enough background so your reader will be able to understand and feel your anxiety. What effect did the stress have on you? What did you do to cope with it? Are you now able to look back on the incident and laugh or do you still feel stress when recalling it?

Reaching (or falling short of) a goal

Have you ever set a goal and stuck with it, overcoming significant obstacles to attain it? Was it ultimately satisfying? Tell about it. Your children and grandchildren know you only as an adult and may see you as someone who has never had to struggle. If you are like most of us, your accomplishments were not predetermined, and your position in life may not be exactly what your children perceive. Help them understand that your successes have been the result of planning and hard work. On the other hand, don't be afraid to tell about the goals you failed to reach. Our lives often turn out differently than we thought they would when we were teenagers. Help your descendants understand that sometimes we have to alter our plans to be successful, or perhaps change our definition of "success."

Standing for something

Have you faced situations where you had to resist pressure to compromise your sense of what was right? Explain why you felt you had to go against the crowd. How did it make you feel when you resisted peer pressure? Have your feelings changed with the passage of time? Have you stubbornly taken a stand when it turned out later you shouldn't have? If so, tell about it. Such stories can prove helpful for young people who will find themselves in similar situations requiring either moral courage or the ability to step back and realize they've been hard-headed and shouldn't resist sound advice.

Learning from mistakes

Have you ever done something you regret, for which you paid consequences, and became a better and wiser person for it? If so, write about it. Don't minimize your mistake or gloss over the difficulties in overcoming it.

Romance

Most people have been in love several times during their lives. You should tell about the people you loved and why you loved them. For people who are married when they write their memoirs, telling about an old girlfriend or a former spouse can be touchy business. You should, of course, try to avoid offending your current spouse. On the other hand, your spouse should understand that you had a life before you met him or her and that you need to feel free to write about it.

In any event, you will want to tell how you met your current love interest and why you fell in love. Where did you go on your first date? Were there bumps in the road? Did you get along with your in-laws? What was your wedding like? Did the happiness outweigh the stress, or vice versa? If you were married for many years, what made the marriage last? If it didn't last, why? What were the most difficult challenges in your marriage? When you and your spouse have disagreements, how do you work these out? How are daily tasks allocated between the two of you? Who makes decisions about what? If a young person were to ask you what to look for in a partner, what advice would you give? If you were to advise newlyweds about how to find happiness in marriage, what would you say?

Military

Were you in the military? If so, give details about when and where you served. Did you enlist, and if so, why? Was military service what you expected it to be? Do you have any good boot camp stories? Were you in combat? Were you wounded? What were your feelings when you saw other soldiers wounded or killed? How did you adapt to the authoritarian nature of the military? Did the military increase or decrease your belief in a divine being? Did you visit any interesting places? If so, be sure to include the setting. On the whole, was the military a positive or negative part of your life? What did you learn from serving your country?

Employment

You will want to tell about the main jobs you have had during your life. Explain what you did in a way that will be understood by people who are not experts in your field. Avoid jargon! Give your draft to someone who knows nothing about your line of work and ask if he finds it confusing or boring. Although this can be sensitive, consider telling, at least in general terms, how much you were paid. Did your pay scale force you to scrimp? Were you fired or laid off, and if so, why? What was the most difficult part of your job? Did you ever have an ethical conflict with your superiors? What choices did you make that influenced your career advancement? Explain what sorts of tools or instruments you used. Chances are when your descendants read your life story, your job either will have ceased to exist or will be done entirely differently. Your descendants will be interested to know how it was done in your day.

For example, when Morris began as an attorney, computers were not yet on the scene. Nor did lawyers do their own typing. Letters were dictated to secretaries. If a secretary made a mistake typing a letter to a client—even a tiny one—the entire page had to be retyped. When computers came into use, they resided only on the secretaries' desks. As lawyers became more competent with computers, electronic databases were created so the attorney could enter a keyword and obtain access to all the relevant statutes and cases in an electronic format, completely changing the nature of legal research and file keeping. It is likely that your profession has seen similarly dramatic shifts toward new technology. Think back on how things were done when you first began working in your field and how you adapted to change.

Your children

If you have children, your relationship with them will probably occupy a central part of your life story. You will want to tell about their births and their contributions to your family. Bear in mind, however, that you are writing *your* memoirs, not your children's. One of our students submitted stories about her adult children in which she played no part. Normally, these sorts of stories do not add much to the parent's reminiscences. If you want to tell your children's complete stories in abbreviated form, consider lumping them together in a chapter near the end of your book or in an appendix. You will definitely want to tell about your interaction with them and your involvement in their lives. How was your life altered because of them? How was it enriched? What sacrifices did you make on their behalf ?

Conflict is a key ingredient in any good story, and children are a fertile source for this kind of material. However, writing about parent-child conflicts can be tricky. Since your children will probably be alive when your memoir is published and may have families of their own, you may not wish to include all of the details about some sorts of clashes. Nevertheless, don't automatically eliminate all parent-child difficulties. If you can present conflicts fairly and with compassion, and if they do not involve disclosing secrets that would be hurtful to your children, consider including them. They will bring color and dimension to your narrative. Just remember to look at the situation through your children's eyes before writing about it. After all, they may have the last word.

Your grandchildren

Grandchildren play an important, but usually subsidiary role in your life as compared to your children. Unless your grandchildren have lived with you for an extended period, they are probably peripheral characters in your story. They can, however, be excellent sources of humor. Since your memoir may have special appeal to your grandchildren and great-grandchildren, you may want to find at least one story about each one that will help illuminate their personalities and your bond with them. For some, of course, this may not be practical. If you have dozens of grandchildren, you'll probably want to choose only the most compelling incidents for inclusion in your memoir.

Tell people the facts and you enlighten their minds, but tell them a story and you touch their souls.
—Jewish proverb

Vacations

What were your most memorable vacations? Be selective here. People will be bored if you merely recite all the places you've been in your life. Pick a few trips that were truly extraordinary and tell stories about what made them so. Who did you share the vacation with? Did it add to your education? Did it increase your understanding of other cultures? Did it prompt you to change the direction of your education or undertake new hobbies? Remember, stories have characters. Did you meet any unusual people? Best-selling author Bill Bryson writes wonderful travel books because he fills them with humorous anecdotes about his traveling companions and memorable people he meets along the way.

Voluntary service

Have you performed volunteer work for your church or community? Have you donated your time to the Boy Scouts, coached a youth softball team, served on the PTA, helped a hospital organization, donated time and funds to the arts, or become involved in political campaigns? Tell how you got involved and describe the rewards and difficulties.

Hobbies

What do you do in your free time? If you are good with your hands, have you made things that can be passed down to your descendants? Tell what attracted you to your hobby and what rewards you have gained from pursuing it. Have you been able to share your hobby with your spouse, a relative, friends? Do you belong to an organization where people share your interest?

Performing arts

Have you performed for others? For instance, do you play an instrument, do you sing or dance, or perform in stage plays or musicals? Tell about your talents, how you developed them, what it was like to overcome stage fright, and how these experiences have enriched and benefitted your life.

Awards and recognitions

If you have won any special awards or achieved any particular recognition, you should explain what sort of effort went into your accomplishment. Here is another opportunity to build suspense. Don't forget to give credit to others who helped you along the way.

Major purchases

We mentioned earlier that you should describe in some detail the houses where you grew up. You may wish to tell about the houses you lived in as an adult, whether you rented or owned and how you selected your neighborhood. What was there about the house that attracted you to it? If cars, boats, or motorcycles are meaningful, tell about them. Was it necessary to budget in order to afford these major purchases? How did you go about it?

Matters that are taboo

Are there important events in your life you feel would be too personal to include? For instance, did you commit a crime? Were you assaulted? Did you have a relationship with someone you don't want others to know about? Would telling this story help illuminate your life if it weren't taboo? If so, consider whether it really would be so bad if others knew about it. We may think our descendants will be shocked by something we have done, when in fact it merely makes us more human. Everyone has failings. Everyone has things they have done (or things done to them) that are embarrassing or regrettable. If, upon reflection, you cannot bring yourself to include something like this in your story, write it up anyway. Put it in a separate place, whether in a file folder or in a secure area of your computer, and let it sit for a while—perhaps months or years. Then go back and read it. You may conclude it wasn't so bad after all. In any event, you will have forced yourself to put the exper-

We may think our descendants will be shocked by something we have done, when in fact it is merely something that makes us more human.

iment down on paper, and often that is the start of a healing process.

Major historic events

What world or local events are worth mentioning? Were there any major news developments that elicited a strong reaction from you at the time? For example, what did you think about the United States invading Iraq? Your descendants will find it fascinating to read your views about events they have studied in school. In Chapter 8 we listed some major events from the past decades. If there are any that produced in you a particularly strong emotion, share them in appropriate places in your story.

Lesser historic events

There are other events that may have been less significant to the world in general but were important to you. You might ask yourself what section you read first when you open a newspaper. Do you read about sports, movies, business, or local issues? If you are a big sports fan, who were your favorite players and why? Who were your favorite movie stars? What books or movies or television shows were particularly memorable for you? You don't need to write extensively about such things; if you're selective and explain why they grabbed your attention, your account will be interesting to readers.

Public figures

Have you interacted on a personal level with any prominent people? Tell how you came to know them and what you thought of them. Your descendants will be especially interested in any "inside scoop" you may have about famous or otherwise notable people.

Religious and spiritual matters

Is religion important to your life? Be sure to explain why or why not. Have you held lay positions in your church or been active in a volunteer ministry? Do you feel you have received spiritual guidance in such endeavors? How has your involvement blessed or complicated your life? For some people, telling about their beliefs will be a significant aspect of their story. For others, it is a sensitive topic that is difficult to broach.

Avoid preachiness. A memoir is a place to be understated and humble.

Our recommendation is that you address religion head on, treating it like any other topic. Still, a word to the wise: Some people have a tendency to attribute nearly everything that has happened to them to divine providence. Such heavy-handedness will be counterproductive in most instances and cause a negative reaction in some readers. The same can be said of stridently anti-religious sentiments. In both cases, we think it's best to lighten up and simply present the facts as you see them, allowing the reader to draw his or her own conclusions about the spiritual matters in your life.

What you have learned

As you write your personal history, you will experience an interesting phenomenon as you discover what your life has been about. Perhaps for the first time you will see yourself as someone on a journey, whose life has had a beginning, a middle, and an end. Of course, you will not be able to write about your death, but your book will have a natural terminus whenever you finish writing.

At some point during the creative process, ask yourself, "What was the shape of my life? What did I learn? Did I develop a credo?" You may want to share some pearls of acquired wisdom with your readers. Of course, it isn't necessary to do this, and in any event you should avoid preachiness. But a quiet explanation of your beliefs will be welcome once readers have gotten to know you. Once again, if you can illustrate your beliefs with stories from your life, the impact will be far greater than if you merely recite what you have learned.

A Final Caveat

We hope you will find this list of writing topics useful. Remember that it is intended only to start your mind working, not as a comprehensive guide. You should write about what was meaningful to you. Your stories do not need to be about earth-shaking events. Some of the very best memoirs have been written by people who never strayed far from home. One of the most popular novelists of all time, Jane Austen, was a homebody. She wrote about what was familiar to her, emphasizing family life and romance. There are no wars or murders in her books. Her novels entertain and resonate with readers because of her insight into human nature, her sparkling dialogue, and her ability to tell a compelling story. You can bring similar tools to your own narrative. Don't feel a need to throw everything you remember into your book. Pick incidents that have the most dramatic promise. It's not how much you tell, but how you tell it that will make your personal history worth reading.

Chapter 13

Breathing on Your Own

Steady to "The End"

J. K. Rowling of Harry Potter fame, the first person ever to become a billionaire by writing books, began her career by penning her first Harry Potter book in a small Edinburgh café during her daughter's naps. She was a single mom with plenty of gumption and a good idea.

Then there's John Grisham, son of Mississippi cotton farmers who had no formal education. Grisham managed to earn a law degree and later established a small private law firm. Inspired by a case he observed in a Mississippi courthouse, Grisham wrote his first novel, *A Time to Kill,* by arriving at his office at five in the morning six days a week and writing for a couple of hours before launching into his legal work.

There's an aura of myth about both of these anecdotes, like most rags to riches stories. However, if we remove the spectacular endings, we're left with a pretty basic plot, one every published—and unpublished—author knows verbatim. It's a tale of sacrifice, dedication, and hard work.

"I write only when I'm inspired. Fortunately, I'm inspired at 9 o'clock every morning."
—William Faulkner

People who want to write, write. They make it a priority, setting aside time to write regularly—no matter whether they have a full-time job or four kids under eight. They sacrifice sleep, leisure time, and other things that get in the way of their craft. They write … no matter what.

Humor writer Patrick McManus says it well. In his introduction to *The Deer on a Bicycle,* he describes the regimen he set for himself when he decided to "get serious" about writing:

> I set up a writing schedule of two hours a day, 7:00 p.m.-9:00 p.m. seven evenings a week, and tried never to miss a single day.

> The writing schedule required that I write for two hours each day—not do research, not read about writing, not think about writing, not make notes about what I intended to write, but actually to pound the keys for a full two hours, whether or not I had anything to write about. I hated it! But after a couple of months of sticking ruthlessly to this schedule, I experienced a peculiar psychological adjustment. Just like Pavlov's dog anticipating the supper bell, but with less drooling, I began to feel a compulsive pull toward the typewriter as seven o'clock approached each night. I could barely wait to get back to whatever story or article I had been working on. Also, I noticed that my writing had become, if not easier, substantially better.[1]

You can always find reasons to procrastinate. There are plenty of excuses, and they can become highly seductive because, let's face it, writing is tough. If you're writing about your life, it can be particularly hard going, fraught with all the emotional hurdles we discussed in Chapter 1.

We have students who sit in class week after week through one course after another. Some write one story per term. Some never write anything. We also have students who bring a new story to class every week because they've made the commitment to do so. Somehow they find the time. The interesting thing is that it doesn't seem to matter how busy the student is. Often those with full-time jobs or children at home are more prolific than retired empty-nesters.

One of Dawn's students began taking her class in January 1999 and started writing his life story on a yellow legal pad. He was obviously focused on his project, turning out stories at a rapid pace. Dawn suggested he make things easier by learning how to use a computer. He did. By April 2004 he had published his third book, utilizing computer skills he had managed to acquire along the way. This man is in his mid-seventies.

Next week or next year always seems like a less stressful and a more convenient time to write. It generally isn't. We never know what challenges lie ahead. One of our wonderful students of several years passed away recently. Fortunately, he had completed and published his life story the previous year. He left his descendants an invaluable legacy, for which they are thankful.

We hope this book has inspired you to pursue your desire to record your experiences on paper. Now you've just got to do it, one page, one story at a time … until it's done.

A Plan for the Perplexed

For those who feel overwhelmed by the magnitude of their project and need a strategy for how to proceed, here are some ideas:

1. If you haven't already done so, complete the Learn by Doing exercises we've presented throughout this book. These exercises will generate a number of stories to set you well on your way, while at the same time introducing you to a variety of writing techniques to enliven your story.

2. Make use of the organizational tools in Chapter 10, which should help you recall incidents and develop a framework for your project. These include creating a chronology (time line) of your life and building a tentative table of contents.

3. Make lists of events, possessions, people, and so on to generate material for story ideas. For example, make a list of:

- all the cars and homes you've owned
- the schools you attended
- major turning points in your life
- influential people in your life
- stories that must be told.

The items in your list should remind you of anecdotes. Pick one and write about it. When you're finished, pick another, and so on. Soon you'll be well into writing your life story.

Learn by Doing

39. Devise a writing schedule that will push you to get your project accomplished. Be specific about the details. Commit, for example, to writing a certain amount of time each day or certain days of each week. Determine when that time will occur and don't let anything interfere. Or as an alternative, consider creating a list of stories that must be written and determine deadlines for completing them. If you don't make a firm commitment, you risk becoming distracted by other activities and all your good intentions coming to nothing.

4. Create a project notebook or other filing system to keep everything pertaining to your project in one place. Add subject dividers and label them according to age (childhood, adolescence, early adulthood), or topic (education, career, vacations), whatever method is most helpful to you. The same system can be replicated on a computer. File your notes and stories under the appropriate category so you can refer to them when you're writing about that period or topic. Every time you think of a new idea, write it down and file it.

5. Try the following memory-triggering exercises to get your creative juices flowing and generate some story ideas:

• Browse through your photo albums. Memories will start flooding back to you. Notice the friends you played with, the vacations you took, the houses you lived in, the furniture in the background, the cars you drove, the pets you owned, the clothes you wore, the way you styled your hair. Jot down story ideas as you go along.

• Look through school annuals. Notice the clubs you belonged to, the sports you played, the dances you attended, the friends and teachers who were important in your life. Read the notes your friends wrote to you on the end pages. Is your mind beginning to reel with memories of the past?

• Look through old scrapbooks and keepsake boxes. Do you have any certificates, trophies, memorabilia, ticket stubs, or letters that trigger memories from the past?

• Call your siblings and other relatives to reminisce. You may find you don't remember incidents in the same way. Visit homes where you lived, schools you

"Success is a finished book, a stack of pages each of which is filled with words. If you reach that point, you have won a victory over yourself no less impressive than sailing single-handed around the world."
—Tom Clancy

attended, cemeteries where loved ones are buried, and other places that have significance in your life. Sit in front of these places for a while and record thoughts that come to you.

6. Take a writing class. Many colleges now offer instruction in life story writing as part of their continuing education program. A class will keep you motivated to write. You'll learn a great deal by listening to stories and comments from other students who are involved in similar projects.

Is It Worth the Effort?

We discussed in Chapter 1 some of the personal rewards awaiting you as you begin writing about your life. As you immerse yourself in your project, you'll develop an enhanced sense of self-worth that comes from realizing you have indeed lived an interesting life. You've survived difficult trials, known and loved wonderful people, and accomplished more than you realized. For us, one of the most rewarding aspects of teaching has been observing how our students come to understand the significance of the lives they've led. What a magnificent discovery!

In addition to these rewards, your personal history will bring your family more pleasure than you can possibly imagine. After publishing histories of some of our ancestors, we've had letters, e-mails, and calls from relatives, their voices brimming with emotion and gratitude for the gift we've given them. Some tell us they now have an increased appreciation for who they are. For instance, one of our sons sent us the following letter after he had read the autobiography of his eighty-six-year-old grandfather, which we had helped bring to fruition:

Dear Dad,

Just wanted to let you know that I read Grandpa's book from cover to cover over the weekend. I was very touched and inspired by his life. I'm so glad that you both took the time to make the book happen. I just feel that it was very important. Not only for Grandpa himself, but for his descendants as well.

It's hard to explain, but while reading about his life, I felt like I was getting to know myself better. Reading about Grandpa gave me a sense of who I was and where I came from. I felt a strong sense of self and pride. I'm glad I was able to read about all those sacrifices he made in his life. Many of those sacrifices benefit me today. I feel extremely grateful to be where I am today, and I now realize, in some small way, I have him (and all my ancestors) to thank.

"If you wait for inspiration, you're not a writer, but a waiter."
—Anonymous

Besides the thoughts expressed above, my other predominant thought while reading Grandpa's memoir was that I hope you and Mom are taking the time to write about your own lives.

You will find that your life stories generate similar responses, resulting in the satisfaction of knowing your efforts have been worthwhile. Knowing this is enough to get started, wouldn't you agree?

Notes

1. Patrick McManus, *The Deer on a Bicycle* (Spokane: Eastern Washington University Press, 2000), 14.

Appendices

A.
Learn-by-Doing exercises

1.   Draw a simple floor plan of your childhood home. If you lived in more than one home, choose the one that was most meaningful to you. First, roughly sketch the exterior walls, then draw in the rooms. Now, begin adding little boxes to represent furniture. Where was your couch located? Your bed? Your kitchen table? Where did your parents place the Christmas tree? Now sketch in the driveway, the garage, prominent trees and shrubs, the tire swing, and so on. (See Appendix B for an example.) You'll find this exercise will resurrect all kinds of memories.

While these thoughts are still fresh in your mind, write a description of this house. Begin with a simple sentence like, "When I was a child, I lived at (fill in address)." Now continue freewriting about that home, including details as they come to you. Don't be content merely to describe the house. Tell how you felt about it. Describe memorable activities that occurred there. If your writing veers off on a tangent, go with it. Later you will come back to this assignment to edit and shape it to your needs. Don't be discouraged if you feel you haven't said what you want to say. You are learning and you will improve with practice.

2. Begin reading a memoir or autobiography that will give you ideas for writing your own life story. (See page 11 for some of our recommendations.) If the book is one you have purchased, underline passages you particularly like. Analyze them to determine what makes them good. Make notes to yourself. Use the book as a training manual. Don't read it all in one sitting. Intersperse your writing with reading. Read the book when you want to relax—when you feel too fatigued to write.

3. Identify a person for whom you feel (or felt) romantic affection. It could be a spouse or a boyfriend or girlfriend. List two or three one-word attributes that attract you to this person. For example, the person may be kind, funny, cheerful, affectionate, intelligent, etc. Recreate an incident involving this person where these attributes are demonstrated. Avoid summary statements like "Jeremy was a cheerful person." Instead, show Jeremy's cheerfulness.

4. Identify a time in your life when you felt afraid. Write a description of how you felt, describing how your body reacted to the incident. What were your thoughts at the time? How did you behave? Show us your feelings, don't just tell about them. For example,

you could describe how you used to duck your head and wish you were elsewhere whenever your mother took you to her hometown and introduced you to her friends and relatives. Or you could dramatize the time you were struck speechless when you suddenly came face to face with the boy you had dreamed about since the first day of school. Or you could let your readers feel your terror when you were asked to deliver a short speech in history class. Describe how the sweat ran down your armpits and your voice trembled, compounding your embarrassment by broadcasting your fear.

5.   Instead of reporting that you grew up in a "small town," take your readers for a walk. Visit the country store and describe the tall glass jars filled with colorful hard candy that attracted you as a child. Look in on the four-room schoolhouse and tell about the classes that consisted of students in several different grade levels. Describe how you could visit any of your friends in town in a few minutes' walk. Write about the telephone operator who knew the names—and much of the business—of every family in town. (Chapter 6 offers more ideas for writing about places.)

6.   Make a list of five to ten life-changing events (turning points) that influenced who you are today. Your list may include such events as moving to a new location, some kind of crisis (a marriage, divorce, illness, death), an achievement, or a chance remark from an acquaintance. For purposes of this assignment, list events that occurred at a specific time and place such as, for instance, the day you decided to get married rather than things that happened over time such as your growth as a person as you adapted to married life.

7. Choose a life-changing event from your list and develop it into a scene. Use dialogue that re-creates emotions you and others felt at that time. Try to avoid a scene with only "talking heads." Give your characters something to do when they speak so readers can visualize real people in a specific setting. For example, a mother dries dishes while she talks to her family. Perhaps she throws down the towel when someone says something that irritates her. Actions like these make the scene feel "real" because we can visualize the incident.

8. Select an event in your life that did not have enormous significance in itself, but illustrates a particular character trait of yours or of another person in your life. Re-create the event as a scene. Use the principle of showing rather than telling so your reader can draw his or her own conclusions.

9. Notice how your body reacts the next time you feel a strong emotion. Write down these reactions for future use. Note how other people display emotions. What happens to their faces and their voices? What do they do with their hands? What other kinds of body language do they display? Write down your observations.

10. Think of a time you were frightened. What kind of behavior did you display? What did you say? Describe

the incident and your reaction to it. Try to be as honest and specific as you can. Let readers feel your fear.

11. Pick an incident in your life when you felt an intense emotion and dramatize that event in a scene. Be honest. Feel the emotion when you're writing. Pour everything out onto the paper in your first draft, then go back and polish it.

12. Read a chapter or two from a novel or one of the memoirs listed in Chapter 1. Notice, in particular, examples that illustrate how the characters reveal their feelings.

13. Now you try it. Select an individual who is noted for something related to his appearance—fastidiousness, slovenliness, or some other attribute. What is it about him that conveys this impression? Be specific. Try placing him in a setting that complements his image—like Russell Baker does in the example cited on page 60.

14. Choose someone you know well. Write a sentence that summarizes one of his or her dominant personality traits, a sentence as simple as, "My sister was a non-stop talker." Now make a list of examples demonstrating the trait. Finally, write a paragraph using these examples. Does he or she come alive on the page?

15. Write about a "crush" you had on someone during your adolescence. Be honest and specific about your feelings. Were you embarrassed? Angry? Shy? Jubilant?

Carefully describe his or her appearance, personality, and behavior. What is it about that person that especially attracted you?

16. Pick an incident from your life that illustrates the personality of someone close to you and re-create that incident in a scene. Try to reconstruct the conversation that occurred. Describe where the incident took place so your readers can visualize the setting.

17. Choose a person who played an important role in your life and write a physical description of that person using specific details that describe her prominent traits. Use more than one sensory clue if you can. What fragrances was this person known for? Is there something notable about the way she talks? Write a quick first draft, then examine your writing, evaluating words and phrases, adding, substituting, deleting, moving phrases around to create different effects.

18. Choose three individuals who will be main characters in your life story. Compose a metaphor or simile to describe a personality trait of each of these characters. (Example: My brother was as lazy as a kite on a windless day.) Try to create a comparison that conveys a vivid image of that trait.

19. Draw a simple map of your hometown, identifying key sites that played a role in your upbringing, such as homes, schools, churches, local hangouts, and recreational sites. What special memories do you have? What

do readers need to know to understand your circumstances there? After you've thought about these questions, write a description of this town that makes it real for your readers.

20. Try capturing the essence of your town in one colorful sentence. Garrison Keillor describes the fictional town of Lake Wobegon in the 1880s with this provocative sentence: "Lake Wobegon was a rough town then, where, all on one block, for less than five dollars, you could get a tattoo, a glass of gin, and a social disease, and have enough left over to get in a poker game, but Lutherans civilized it."

Here's how one of our students completed this assignment: "I grew up in a Wisconsin town so small you could—with one vigorous sneeze—miss sight of the cows, banks, service stations, and U-Need-A-Lunch diner and find yourself on the town's outskirts, hungry and out of gas."

21. Write a description that leads your reader on a "tour" of your community. If people were to drive into your town, what would they see first? What landmarks would catch their attention? What sights, sounds, and smells would they notice?

22. Describe what it was like to be a teenager in the town where you spent your adolescence. What did you do for fun? Where were the hangouts? What slang expressions were popular? What did you like and dislike about the town at that time? What made your town dif-

"Everyone who has ever taken a shower has had an idea. It's the person who gets out of the shower, dries off, and does something about it that makes a difference."
—Nolan Bushnell

ferent from others? Capture the atmosphere with specific details.

23. Write a story about the role of radio or television in your home life. What programs did you enjoy? What did the early radios (or televisions) look like? What stations were available? Are there any amusing anecdotes you can tell that will give your readers a sense of what your home was like at that time?

24. Describe the way you dressed and wore your hair when you were in high school. Be specific so the era comes alive. Did you wear clothing that was "in fashion"? What influenced what you wore? How did you feel about the way you looked? The way others looked?

25. Choose an historical event that occurred during your lifetime and explain how it influenced your life. How involved were you with the event? How did you feel about it? Have your feelings changed? Did it affect the choices you made, then or later? Tell enough about it so future generations can grasp what happened, but be careful not to launch into an encyclopedic account that loses track of your story.

26. Many people divide their personal histories into "chapters" that begin with a major change in their life—a relocation, marriage, career advancement, career change, or religious conversion. Select a potential chapter in your life story and write an introduction incorporating the historical events that may have affected your changed circumstances. Think hard about this one—

don't blithely dismiss the possibility that the change was sparked by outside influences. If necessary, spend time in the library or on the Internet learning more about the history of the time and place.

27. List five historical events or developments that have affected your life. Select one and write a paragraph or two explaining how it influenced or changed you and how you felt about it.

28. Do you know anyone who might be considered famous within certain circles? Write about your relationship. Explain what you thought about the person and how he or she affected you.

29. Write about when you needed something badly— money, a job, an honor or award, the recognition of another person. Carefully describe what you did. Reveal what was at stake and what emotions you experienced. Lead your reader through the entire episode, identifying roadblocks and looking for ways to build suspense. Choose strong verbs that intensify the tension. Don't telegraph the outcome.

30. Write about a time when you or someone you cared about was in danger. Re-create the incident as it happened, including specific details to heighten your readers' worry about the outcome.

31. Review one of your stories for any non-essential clutter that can be eliminated. Does every sentence add to the story? Are there any paragraphs that can be shortened or deleted? Can stronger and more unique nouns and verbs eliminate some of those superfluous adjectives and adverbs? Be ruthless in your editing. Don't let your ego sabotage good writing.

32. Choose one of the stories you've already written and try shortening it by half. Has the story suffered by being shortened, or has it been improved?

33. Many stories lack the punch that grabs a reader because the author has taken too long getting it started. Examine the introductions to each of the stories you've written. Do any of them linger too long on unnecessary details or back-story? Notice where the action begins. If this point is far down on the page, move it closer to the top by rearranging or eliminating some of your own paragraphs.

34. Get more organized. Create a list of stories that must be told. Make a tentative table of contents. Begin compiling a life chronology.

35. If you have completed most of the exercises in this book, you are ready to try writing a beginning for your life story. Review the questions on page 153. Make a list of possible ways to begin. Experiment with different approaches. Read two or three of your favorites out loud and see which one grabs you.

36. Select an incident or event that represents a high point or turning point for you and tell the story from

beginning to end. Read what you've written, find the story's climactic moment, and consider beginning your story at that point. Will it grab your readers' attention?

37.   Write your beginning as a scene, as Marjorie Carter does earlier in Chapter 11. Put words in the mouths of your characters and let them talk to each other. Bring them to life by giving them something to do when they talk. Let your readers "see" the setting where the scene occurs.

38.   If you have completed Exercise 6, you already have a list of five to ten life-altering events that must be part of your history. As you read through Chapter 12, whenever you think of a story that might be included in your history, describe the event in a summary sentence or two. When you are finished with the chapter, you should have a considerably longer list of potential stories. Look it over and assign a ranking to each one based on how interesting you feel the story will be to your readers, perhaps designating those with the most potential with the number "1" and those with the least potential with a "3." Write up the pieces with the most potential first. From this core list, you can progress through much of your life story. Refer back to the list as you continue to write.

39.   Devise a writing schedule that will push you to get your project accomplished. Be specific about the details. Commit, for example, to writing a certain amount of time each day or certain days of each week. Determine when that time will occur and don't let anything interfere. Or as an alternative, consider creating a list of stories that must be written and determine deadlines for completing them. If you don't make a firm commitment, you risk becoming distracted by other activities and all your good intentions coming to nothing.

B.

Sample sketch of a childhood home

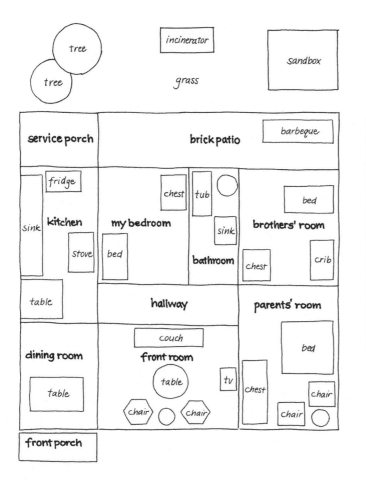

See **Learn by Doing Exercise 1**. This is a rendering of Dawn's childhood home. Try drawing a sketch of all of your homes. The task will resurrect all kinds of memories and help you write more vividly about these important places. Consider including your drawings as visual aids in your finished story.

195

C.

Sample sketch of a neighborhood

The image on the following page is a map of the small town of Annabella, Utah. The map was based on a hand-drawn sketch prepared by Morris' father, who was born there. The map shows the locations of public buildings that existed in the early decades of the twentieth century (the Post Office, Recreation Hall, "Old Church," "Old Schoolhouse," "New Schoolhouse"). It also shows where Morris' father (E. Elroy Thurston) was born, the house of his grandfather (Edwin T. Thurston), and the houses of various aunts and uncles who played a part in his early life.

See **Learn by Doing** *Exercise 19.*

When you prepare a map of your neighborhood, you'll probably want to start with a hand-drawn sketch, which is a good tool to help bring back memories. If you eventually want a more formal look, you (or your children) can easily convert your sketch into a more precise computer-drawn sketch using mapping software or an on-line mapping service.

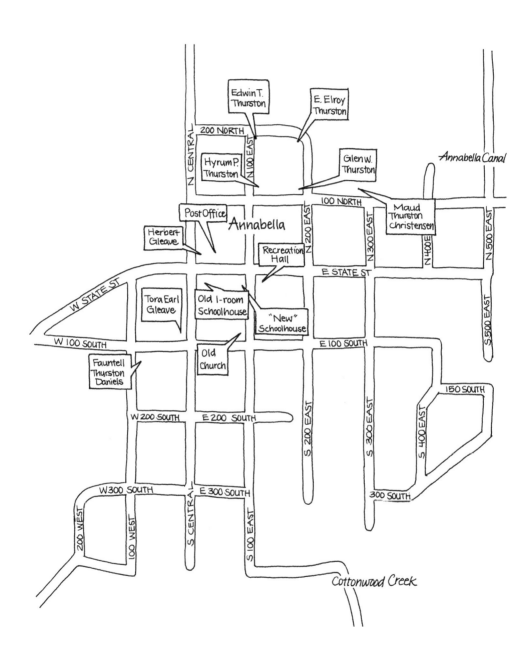

D.

Award-winning stories

We've mentioned how proud we are of our students who have completed their personal histories, many of whom have continued to write about incidents in their lives and had their stories published. The following essays demonstrate, better than anything else we could say, what we consider to be well-written stories—real excellence in writing. Both were composed by students in Dawn's Advanced Life Story Writing class at Santiago Canyon College. The first, by Bonnie Copeland, appeared in Beth Maltbie Uyehara's anthology, *Celebrating Family History*, published in 2005 by the Southern California Genealogy Society (SCGS), which awarded it a First Place, Long Category award. The second, by Willie Walker, won Third Place, Short Category, in the 2006 SCGS competition.

Bonnie reports that writing her life story has made her realize how deeply she cares for her family and how much they've given her. In the story below, she writes about a chilly winter evening in West Virginia, capturing a sense of place so well we feel we're right there with her shivering in the night air. She says of this story: "I write about West Virginia to understand. The two years I spent there have haunted me ever since I left. Thirty years later, I wake up at night and feel I'm still there. I look around, expecting to see reflected light from the coal furnace in the living room flickering on the pine boards of the hall. I'd like to know why, so I write about it."

Willie's stories emanate from his nostalgia for a boyhood spent among simple, hard-working poor folks in rural southern Alabama. His stories feel real and true, and when he reads them in Dawn's classes in his rich Southern accent, he leaves an emotional imprint on his listeners. He explains that he writes "because there is a tiny voice in my soul that tells me if I don't, something of value will be lost to those who may care. I hope to leave some record of that space and time I had the good fortune to be part of and to honor people and a way of life that should not be forgotten."

Sistersville Saturday Night
Bonnie Copeland

THERE IS NO MIST on the river this evening. The air is cold and clear; the water is still as glass. I can see two Big Dippers, one in the sky and one in the river below. Waves sigh like sleeping babies as they break on the shore beneath my kitchen window.

Far off, silhouetted against the reflection of the moon on the water, the Sistersville Ferry glides between Ohio and West Virginia. In the 160 years since 1817, a Harmon has ferried wagons and cows and pigs and cars and foot passengers from one side of the river to the other, moving back and forth, six a.m. to six p.m., four trips an hour, seven days a week, April 1st through Christmas Eve. In the old days, Dib Harmon told me, the river was shallow enough for his great-grandpa to pole all the way across. Today he only uses the pole to maneuver near the ferry landing; it takes a diesel engine to get through the current and past the shipping lanes dredged into the middle of the river. Things change very slowly here in the Ohio River Valley, but they still change.

I can barely see the ramshackle building across the river, but I know it houses the tackle and bait shop, post office, and cafe that constitute the city center of Fly, Ohio. The building is only a purple shadow, but the red neon sign on top illuminates the night sky like Las Vegas lights up the desert. The river is too wide for me to read the sign but I can translate it from the backward cipher reflected by the water. "Fly Café — The Best Pie and We Don't Lie" shimmers in the black river and shatters into a million rubies as the ferry cuts through it.

Even though it's dark, it's only five p.m. The Fly Café is open until six on Saturday and the ferry runs until six, but the A&P market in Sistersville closed an hour ago. We haven't had dinner yet, and there's nothing in the refrigerator. The frost crunches under my bare feet as I step out onto the wooden porch. I cup my hands and call into the darkness, "Shannon! It's mother. Come home. We're going to Fly for take-out!"

A grimy seven-year-old appears out of the darkness. "Get your hat," I say, "and put on your galoshes. And for heaven's sake, wash your face. You look like you've been playing in the chicken yard again."

Shannon titters and hides a guilty smile behind a grimy hand. She goes inside to wash up at the kitchen sink. I follow her into the kitchen, where I've left my parka draped over a chair. I put on my parka and rubber boots and grab my mittens and purse. I scrape the hoarfrost off of the windshield of our red Volkswagen and we head north on Rural Route 2 toward the Mason-Dixon Line and the ferry landing.

The ferry is waiting for us when we get to Wells Landing. I park our car under the shadow of the old oil well in Wells Landing Park and we wade through the mud to the ferry. I pay for our passage with two dimes that Dib slips into the silver coin changer at his waist.

"Hah," says Dib for the umpteenth time. "It's the pretty sistahs from Sistahsville, Wes' Virginia."

"She's my mother," Shannon says in disgust.

Dib's eyes twinkle and his teeth flash in the dark. "Oh. Looks young enough to be yo' sistah. And you look old enough to have a sistah her age, young lady. You do."

Shannon's frown turns into a smile. She can't wait to grow up.

Even though we're the only people on the ferry, Dib announces, "Passengers take theah seats. Ship ahoy!"

Shannon and I take a seat on the damp bench facing West Virginia. I put my arm around her to keep her warm. Dib lifts his pole from its hooks on the railing and carefully plants it in the water. The ferry pivots around the pole until we are facing our destination, Ohio.

Dib climbs into the pilot house, pokes his arm out of

the window, and tugs on a rope. A single ear-splitting "broouch" explodes from the whistle. The diesel engine shudders and the ferry leaps forward. The smell of diesel fuel mixes with the cold air. I hold on to Shannon with one hand and the railing with the other so we aren't jerked into the water.

Ten feet out, the river closes in on us. Chill air wraps us like an ice cream cloak. I feel as if I cannot move. One arm is holding Shannon and the other is pinned to the rail. Even the "putt-putt" of the diesel is muffled by the heavy dampness. Wind reaches under my hat and caresses my hair. My cheeks are numb with cold; my eyelids burn. Tears freeze to my lashes and form a crystalline curtain between me and the rest of the world. The Sistersville Ferry slips into the moonlight as if it were moving into a dream.

Sometimes in the morning I ride the ferry to work instead of driving twelve miles upriver to the New Martinsville Bridge. My eyes water in the cold. On winter mornings the mountains on both sides of the river are shrouded by fog; the spindly tree skeletons that cover them float in my tears like ghostly apparitions. I exhale white puffs that disappear into the heavy mist, like the roads and buildings on the river banks. The fog is so thick I cannot see my hands. I am surrounded by the faint odor of fish and wet leaves. It is as if time has stopped, and I can imagine that the river looks the same as it did a hundred years ago.

With a bump and a thud the ferry scrapes against the mud flat of Fly landing. Shannon and I get off and slog across the frozen tire ridges toward the café. Our path is lit by Fly's single street lamp and the red blush from the sign on the roof. A piece of plywood nailed to a wooden lamp post by the side of the road announces, "Fly Café—The Best Pie and We Don't Lie," but the light over it has been burned out for years.

Dib shouts, "Gitcher food to go. This'll be mah last trip tonight … I'll wait fuh you."

Shannon sits and waits in the grey skeleton of a wooden rocker. She knows that it'll take me a few minutes to open the front door.

I struggle with the warped door. It pops open. The warm air and light that pour out almost knock us over. I smell the blend of damp old building, burning wood from the pot-bellied stove, trucker sweat, the river and food … glorious food!

We pass the tables with their red and white checkered oilcloth covers and seat ourselves on chrome stools in front of the yellow Formica counter. Ella, the owner and waitress, slides a pencil from under her pink hairnet and asks, "Whad' ya gonna have?"

I ignore the stained menus in the metal holders at the rear of the counter. Instead, I check the chalkboard on the wall. Some of the specials are gone, erased from the board, but I can still read them. Earlier we could have had pot roast and gravy or homemade meat loaf or fresh river fish, fried Cajun-style. I would have liked to have the fish, but people in Appalachia learn to live with disappointment. What's gone is gone.

"I'll have the roast turkey with mashed potatoes, gravy, and the fresh baked beets, to go, please," I say. "And could you put the rolls in a separate bag so we can eat them on the ferry?"

"You'll need extra rolls if'n you took the ferry," Ella says. She wipes her hands on the sides of her pink uniform and turns to Shannon. "Whad'll it be fuh you, li'l honey?"

Shannon doesn't have to look at the menu to know what she wants. She only eats one main dish. "Macaroni and cheese," she says, "to go."

Ella carves the turkey and covers the bottom of a metal pie plate with it. She plops two scoops of mashed potatoes on top of the turkey, dumps a scoop of corn bread dressing onto the potatoes, adds a spatula full of butter, pours gravy over everything and sets the pan aside. Then she places the remaining six roasted beets onto a doubled sheet of tin foil and wraps them up. "Gave yuh all the beets," she says. "We'll be switchin' tuh corn tomorrow."

She ladles macaroni and cheese into another pie pan. The cheese stretches in long strings from the baking dish. Ella finally upends the baking dish and scrapes the last of the macaroni and cheese into the pie pan. She covers both pans with tin foil and secures the foil with gum bands.

Now she turns to us with the big question. "What kinda pie yuh gonna have?" Pie is included with dinner, and the Fly Café always has at least twenty-one flavors. I am torn between lemon meringue, chocolate cream, and Dutch apple with cheddar crust. The peach pie looks good, too, but this time of year it's probably made from canned peaches. I think I'll wait until spring for peach, but the rhubarb looks fresh, and so does the cherry.

"The raspberry is the same raspberries we had in the fall," Ella says. "Froze 'em. Pies'r jus' finished, still warm. Took 'em out at five o'clock."

"I'll have the raspberry," I say decisively, "and a cup of black coffee for Dib."

Shannon doesn't even have to order her pie. Ella already knows that banana cream is the only kind she'll eat.

Everything is double-bagged in brown paper sacks and I pay $4.45 at the register. Shannon carries the bag with the pie in it and I carry the dinners and the warm rolls and Dib's coffee across the frozen tire tracks to the waiting ferry.

The wind has picked up some. The air temperature has dropped and mist has begun to rise from the river. There's a new passenger on the ferry, a man we do not know, with a brand-new 1977 Ford Fairlane.

Dib collects the fare, two dimes from me and sixty cents from the stranger. He unties the rope and pushes the ferry away from the dock with the pole. The ferry drifts into the current. He stabs the pole into the mud at the bottom of the river and grunts with the effort of holding it steady in the stronger current on the Ohio side. Slowly, the ferry pivots around the pole until we are facing West Virginia. Dib places the pole back in the hooks on the railing.

I open the bag of rolls and a sweet yeasty smell swirls around my face. I hand out the warm rolls—one for Shannon, one for the stranger, and one for me. I give Dib his roll and coffee. He stuffs the entire roll into his mouth and drains the cup with a single swig.

Dib carries his empty cup into the pilot house. The diesel engine springs to life. He reaches out of the window and tugs twice on the rope. Shannon covers her ears as the horn blows "broouch, broouch."

The warm bags of food rest against my legs as I wrap

one arm around the railing and one around Shannon to keep her from falling off of the boat.

The red neon sign on top of the building goes dark. The words, "Fly Café — The Best Pie and We Don't Lie" dissolve into the river. We follow the moonlight toward home.

Ode to That Little Brown Shack Out Back
Willie Walker

> Oh, it was not so long ago,
> That I went trippin' through the snow,
> Out back behind my old hound dog.
> There I'd sit me down to rest,
> Like a snowbird on its nest,
> And read the Sears and Roebuck catalog.
>
> —*Billy Edd Wheeler*

I DRIED MY FACE AND looked into the mirror. Looking back at me was the face of an old man surrounded by a modern bathroom with polished chrome fixtures, colorful ceramic marbled Italian tile, decorator fluorescent lights, glossy clean white cabinets, and frosted glass shower door. They were pleasant to look at, things that cost a small fortune, even though I did all the work. They meant little to me now. Just some of the necessities of life. The toilet flushes effectively. Lavender air fresheners caress my nostrils. Sanitizers keep the bacteria count down to healthful levels. The temperature is always comfortable.

"Wilburn, where are you?" my wife yells from the patio.

For an instant, memories flood back.

"Wilburn, where are you?" I remember a young mother calling from the porch of an old unpainted farm house and her sandy-haired son hiding in a small outdoor privy with a pretty blue-eyed girl seven years old with blonde curls and a cherubic face.

At age five, he knew he was in real trouble.

"I gotta go, Frankie," he whispered. "Momma will whup me."

"No, stay still till she goes inside."

Both pressed noses to the unpainted boards and watched through cracks as his momma came down the porch steps and walked slowly toward their hiding place. He was caught. There was no way out. Visions filled his head of being held by his left wrist while justice was meted out with a peach tree switch. When his momma turned to look back at the farm house, he ran out the outhouse door for the cover of the tall cotton stalks in the field behind the privy. Once in the middle of the field, he hid and tried to think of a way out of his predicament.

It was not his fault, of course. He was young and innocent. It was Frankie's fault. She was always wanting to hide somewhere and play show and tell and getting him in trouble. He pouted. Her momma only laughed when his momma told on them.

"Pearl, don't worry about it," she said. "They're just little young 'uns."

An only child, Frankie was precocious, spoiled, and used to getting her way. Her daddy owned the land his daddy share-cropped and her parents worshipped her.

"Wilburn, it will be worse for you if you don't come here right now."

He knew it was true. Reluctant and snuffling, he started for the peach tree in the backyard of the farm house to choose the smallest switch he thought his momma would accept.

Down a dirt path, pounded and packed like concrete by thousands of hurried footsteps and lined by wildflowers that Momma had planted, stood that small weathered brown privy that looms large in my memory. It was a private place where there was seldom a latch on the door and only one of the multiple holes was ever in use at any one time. There, on a lazy summer's day, a boy could dream and commune with nature in the form of a buzzing green blowfly or a black widow spider industriously building a web—a boudoir for a tiny male lover whose last act of love was to give his life to his mate as she devoured him for being so driven by instinct to procreate. Fear of the spiders tended to make insecure users of the place squat with their feet on the seat. A piece of paper on fire usually chased the critters away.

There one could dream of owning all those wondrous things in the Sears and Roebuck catalog, though the photos of women wearing undergarments were always thoughtfully removed by mothers of sons.

The lower back portion of the building was open to facilitate shoveling a covering layer of soil occasionally. This opening allowed cold wintry winds to blow forcefully up through the wooden seat, where one must sit exposed, making reading and daydreams impossible. That frigid experience would be followed by a fast run back up the path to the house to stand as close as possible with one's backside to the blazing fire in the fireplace.

On rainy days, the sound of the rain pelting on the sheet metal roof was a symphony that could lull one to sleep.

Sometimes it was necessary to move the structure. A pit was dug in the red clay of the Alabama earth. The little building was pulled by mules to its new location and a fresh start was made. The old location was covered over by a thick layer of earth, possibly providing future bottle collectors and scientists an exciting repository for bits of historical artifacts that may have been deposited there.

It was a favorite thing for teenage boys to get even with someone by tipping the toilet over. Most farmers were good-natured about such shenanigans, but some were apt to shoot a load of rock salt into the backside of anyone they caught messing around their private privy unannounced.

Lest I in anyway sound as if I'm romanticizing that peculiar "necessary" of a bygone age, please know that it was not in the slightest a romantic place. It was a place known to spread diseases, such as parasites, typhoid, and other virulent illnesses via flies, soil, and water well contamination. During the heat of summer, it stunk to high heaven, but it was the only thing available to poor people who had very few resources to better the situation.

After writing these few memories, I realize why I have put so much money and attention into my present-day bathrooms: I didn't much like outhouses.

Index

Snoopy, 24, 137

Southey, Robert, 161

Spellbound, 119

Steinbeck, John, 7

story ideas, 155-172

Thurston, Morris (Sr.), 102-04, 131-32

Twain, Mark, 21, 54, 127

Walker, Willie, 82-83, 200, 207-10

West, Jessamyn, 175

Wilde, Oscar, 128

Wodehouse, P. G., 140

Wolfe, Thomas, 130

Wolff, Tobias, 11, 48, 56-57

Wordsworth, William, 43

writing (about): accidents and illnesses, 161-62; ancestors, 156-57; antagonists, 159; awards and recognition, 168-69; birth, 143, 157-58; childhood home, 14, 148, 195; children, 166-67; difficult subjects, 51-53, 169-70; employment, 165-66; fear, 23; feelings, 41-51; friends and relatives, 158-59; goals, 163; hobbies, 168; houses where you lived, 158, 195; humorous incidents, 162; ideals, 163; illnesses and accidents, 161- 62; military service, 164-65; mistakes, 43-44, 163-64; near-death experiences, 162; parents, 157; purchases, 169; romance, 164; school, 159-60; spirituality, 171; stressful experiences, 162-63; summer jobs, 160-61; talents and performing arts, 168; vacations, 167-68. *See also* disclaimers, history, neighborhood, pop culture, setting

writing techniques: cutting clutter, 125-37; descriptive forms, 17-20, 57-60, 128-30; dialogue, 32-37, 71-72; freewriting, 9; "gut level," 41-51; memory triggers, 177-78; personalizing a place, 76-84; prompts, 155-72; reading, 10, 14; schedules, 174-78, 193; sensory cues, 58-59, 82-83; showing (not telling), 15-22, 63-73, 119-20; streamlining, 130-37; suspense, 113-23; write first, polish later, 8. *See also* character development, life story, metaphors, realism, scenes,

Zinsser, William, 42, 80, 95, 110, 160

About the Authors

You might expect Dawn and Morris Thurston to have some shared interests after forty years of marriage—and you would be right. Perhaps their most consuming mutual passion is researching and writing about their ancestors, an interest they took up the year they were married. Even though they were financially challenged college students, when they took a genealogy course together and caught the spirit of it, they borrowed from food money for a trip to Salt Lake City's Family History Library. As their store of information grew, they came to understand that lives are best remembered through stories that move beyond mere names and dates.

Decades later, the Thurstons are now recognized teachers and lecturers, having tutored thousands of people in the art of personal history writing. They are mentors and cheerleaders, helping students write stories that resonate with others—stories that strive to be more than travelogues or family trees in sentence form.

Much has happened since those early days of their marriage. After putting her studies on hold to support her husband through law school, Dawn returned to academia. Two children later, she received a BA in English (with honors) from UCLA, and when their four children were grown, she attended California State University, Fullerton, and earned an MA in communications. She has taught writing for more than a decade at Santiago Canyon College in Orange County, California, and is quick to brag about her students who have gone on to publish their own books and win prizes in writing contests. More recently she has taught courses at the University of Utah. She frequently lectures at family history and continuing education conferences and enjoys speaking to writing support groups. In addition to her published articles in newspapers and professional journals, she has to her credit a book-length treatment of her Scottish grandparents: *Remembering William Miller and Bella Bullock Miller.*

Besides teaching and writing, Dawn and Morris share several other interests in common, such as an enthusiasm for travel, literature, history, and movies. Of course, they have their individual interests. Morris enjoys sports and photography, while Dawn finds cooking and gardening more captivating. "She watches Martha Stewart; I watch the Lakers," Morris observes.

Morris began his collegiate studies at Brigham Young University, then earned a JD degree from Harvard Law School. He went on to become a senior partner with the global law firm of Latham & Watkins, specializing in copyright and trademark matters. Currently he is an adjunct professor at BYU's Law School, as well as a volume editor for the prestigious Joseph Smith Papers Project. In addition to publishing articles in legal and historical journals, he wrote

Tora Thurston: The History of a Norwegian Pioneer, an ancestral biography that won first prize in the Dallas Genealogical Society's national writing contest. He has also edited his father's autobiography and contributed a chapter to *Lives of the Saints: Writing Mormon Biography and Autobiography*. He frequently lectures with Dawn on life story writing.

Dawn and Morris live in Villa Park, California.

––––––––––––––

Illustrator Amy Reeder Hadley grew up in Colorado and got her start by placing in Tokyo Pop's "Rising Stars of Manga" international contest. She is currently working for Tokyo Pop on a three-part manga drama called *Fool's Gold* and has other projects in development with DC Comics. She is a Brigham Young University graduate.